The Living Waters Series

Drenched in Faith

The Transformative Act of Water Baptism

By Lori Ann Moeszinger

Memoir
When Death Knocked at My Door:
The 5 Moments that Changed My Life

Autobiography
Total Surrender: My Story
and Your Blueprint for a Meaningful Life

Christian Living
Passion for Christ: New Beginnings

The Living Waters Series
Faith On Trial: The Startling Reality of Genuine Belief

Drenched in Faith: The Transformative Act of Water Baptism

Spirit Filled Life: The Unseen Force of Divine Power

The Bible Unbound: Trust, Translation, and Transformation

Prophets and Pulpits: Discerning Truth in the House of God

Beyond the Tithe: The Transformative Power of Generous Faith

Heart of Abundance: The Journey to Radical Giving and Receiving

Heaven's Reach: Drawing the Unbelieving into the Fold

Breaking Silence: The Charge to Uphold the Faith Out Loud

Beyond the Final Breath: The Christian's Voyage into Eternity

Christian Living
In Sacred Conversation: The New Testament Prayer Guide

The Living Waters Series

Drenched in Faith
The Transformative Act of Water Baptism

By

Lori Ann Moeszinger

THE RIDGE

PUBLISHING GROUP

The Ridge Publishing Group
Coeur d'Alene, Idaho, U.S.A.

CREDIT: This book was written with limited assistance of ChatGPT, an AI language model developed by OpenAI. The collaboration provided unique insights and support in crafting content. The book cover was created using Adobe Photoshop, ensuring a visually captivating infographic and design.

Library of Congress Control Number: 2024920979

Drenched in Faith: The Transformative Act of Water Baptism / by Lori Ann Moeszinger

ISBN: 978-1-956905-26-7 (e-book)
ISBN: 978-1-956905-25-0 (softcover)

1. Religion / Christian Living / General. 2. Religion / Christian Living / Spiritual Growth. 3. Religion / Christian Life / Inspirational. 4. Religion / Christian Life / Personal Growth. 5. Religion / Christian Living / Social Issues. I. Title. II. Title Series

First Edition: October 2024

Printed in the United States of America

Contents

The Living Waters Series invites readers to rediscover the transformative power of faith. These books open the door to a renewed understanding of devotion, exploring the foundational truths of Christianity with fresh insights and heartfelt sincerity. Whether you are at the start of your spiritual journey or seeking to deepen your faith, these books offer guidance, inspiration, and a renewed sense of connection with Christ.

Join Our Community

Dive deeper into your faith and join a community of like-minded believers by connecting with us across multiple platforms:

- **Facebook Page**: Follow us at Guardians of Biblical Truth to stay updated with inspirational content and community discussions.
- **Facebook Group**: Join our closed group, Guardians of Biblical Truth Forum, for more personal interactions, where you can share, discuss, and grow in your understanding of biblical truths.
- **Blog**: Visit our blog at Jesus-Says.com for thoughtful posts, devotionals, and biblical interpretations aimed at nurturing your spiritual growth.
- **Social Media**: Connect with us on X and Instagram @NNSBible and Pinterest @GuardiansOfBiblicalTruth to get daily inspirations and engage with a community that values deep, scriptural truths.

We look forward to connecting with you and growing together in faith!

The Living Waters Series

Drenched in Faith
The Transformative Act of Water Baptism

Introduction

What Does It Mean to Be a Real Christian?

Welcome to The Living Waters Series—an awe-inspiring and transformative pilgrimage into the heart of the Christian faith. These pages are an invitation to embark on a spiritual odyssey, a quest to fathom the profound depths of our devotion, and an opportunity to dive headfirst into the majestic mysteries that have shaped our spiritual heritage.

In the second chapter of our series, "Drenched in Faith: The Transformative Act of Water Baptism," we are about to embark on an exhilarating journey—one that promises to take us through the crystalline waters of baptism, a time-honored sacrament that has been an ever-flowing river of grace, cleansing the souls of believers, marking new beginnings, and stirring the depths of faith for countless generations. In the following chapters, we will delve into the labyrinthine layers of its rich history, explore the multilayered symbolism it bears, and seek to understand the profound and enduring relevance it holds in the tapestry of our Christian walk.

But remember, this odyssey is not a solitary expedition confined within the boundaries of a book. It is an ever-unfolding adventure, a river of faith that courses its way through the pages of our lives. The Living Waters Series serves as a tribute to the spiritual currents that sustain us, the timeless truths that inspire us, and the boundless grace that beckons us ever closer to the heart of God.

So, as you embark on this literary voyage, may your heart be wide open, your spirit unquenchably eager, and your faith irresistibly drawn to be drenched in the living waters of divine revelation. With each turn of the page, let us explore the fathomless depths, navigate the currents of inspiration, and emerge transformed by the unyielding power of faith's enduring flow. Together, we shall dive deeper into the river of our faith, letting its currents carry us further into the heart of the Divine, where the waters of grace and revelation await us with open arms.

The Living Waters Series: An Ongoing Expedition

As we set forth on this sacred journey, it's essential to acknowledge that this is not a finite exploration contained within the pages of a single book. Instead, it's a perpetual quest, an ongoing expedition into the profound depths of faith and spirituality. The Living Waters Series is an ever-flowing river, winding its way through the landscape of our souls, nourishing our spirits, and guiding us to new revelations with every bend in the stream.

In "Drenched in Faith," we will wade into the waters of baptism, a spiritual river that has quenched the thirst of countless souls and washed away the stains of sin. We'll immerse ourselves in its history, its symbolism, and its role in our Christian journey. But let us remember that this exploration is just one tributary of a much larger river—an exploration that will continue to unfold in future books of the series.

For example, our next destination, "Spirit Filled Life: The Unseen Force of Divine Power," will lead us even further into the mysteries of faith, as we delve into the transformative work of the Holy Spirit. It is an invitation to explore the unseen, the ethereal, and the transcendent—a chance to experience the divine force that propels our faith journey forward.

And beyond that lies a horizon filled with more revelations, deeper understandings, and the boundless grace of God. The Living Waters Series is a testament to our unquenchable thirst for spiritual growth, our unending search for truth, and our unwavering faith in the living God.

So, as we venture into the pages of "Drenched in Faith," remember that this is not merely a book; it is a tributary of an endless river, a thread in the tapestry of our spiritual expedition.

With each book, we draw nearer to the source of living water, and with each page, we drink deeply from the wellsprings of faith.

May your heart be a vessel for these living waters, your soul a canvas for divine revelation, and your spirit a beacon for others seeking to navigate the currents of faith. The journey has begun, dear reader, and it is an adventure like no other—one that beckons you to be drenched in the transformative power of faith's enduring flow.

Invitation

After reading this far, I thank you. With that said, I never start a book without giving an opportunity for people to get right with God. It is really inescapable, the fact that the Bible does teach eternity—once we are born, we live forever. There really is a heaven. There really is a hell. And the Bible tells us that we are going to spend eternity in one of these two places. The choice is ours. God has already made His choice. God loves us. He sent His only Son, Jesus Christ, to die on a cross for the forgiveness of our sins.

> "For God so loved the world, that He gave His only begotten Son, Jesus Christ, that whosoever believes in Him should not perish (cease to exist) but have everlasting life" (John 3:16).

Because God is holy, we need to be holy through Jesus Christ; He will never change, He is immutable, unchangeable. He is in the total state of sinless perfection in everything that He does. But you and I are not holy. By nature, we are sinful and selfish. And because we are sinful and selfish, we are separated from a holy God. But God told us, we were created in His image, and it is His desire to redeem us to right relationship with Him. Therefore, Jesus is the bridge between the holiness of God and the unholiness of humanity. And the Bible also tells us that the only way to break the curse of sin and to find right relationship with God is through Jesus Christ.

"Jesus says unto him, I am the way, the truth, and the life: no man comes unto the Father, but by Me" (John 14:6).

The Gospel

The word "gospel" in the Greek original text means "good news of the kingdom of God." In Christianity, the term "good news" refers to the story of Jesus Christ's birth, ministry, death, and resurrection. Jesus Christ, the Son of God, died for our sins and rose again, eternally triumphant over His enemies—so that there is now no condemnation for those who believe but only everlasting joy. Wherefore the fullness of the gospel is in God Himself—enjoyed by His redeemed people.

Through the death, the ministry, the burial, and the resurrection of Jesus Christ, you and I not only have power over sin, but we have power over sickness, disease, and infirmity—yesterday, today, and forever. The same seven ways Jesus healed in the New Testament are still available to every believer today. Jesus Christ is still the great physician, and no weapon formed against His children shall prosper in the name of the Lord Jesus Christ.

> "But He was wounded for our transgressions (sins), He was bruised for our iniquities (immoral behavior): the chastisement (punishment) of our peace was upon Him; and with His stripes (the marks on His back from His beating) we are healed" (Isaiah 53:5).

> "Who His own self bore our sins in His own body on the tree (cross), that we being dead to sins, should live unto righteousness: by whose stripes you are healed" (1 Peter 2:24).

Making Peace with God

How do you make peace with God?

You have to do two things:

First, you must believe in the gospel—the teaching and revelation of Christ. The gospel, just as the Scripture says: (1) Jesus Christ, God the Father's only Son, lived on this Earth, (2) died on a cross for the forgiveness of our sins, (3) was buried, (4) was raised from the dead on the third day, (5) stayed on this planet for 40 days before ascending to heaven, (6) promised to return, and (7) we are saved by faith alone in Christ alone—this is called the doctrine of salvation.

Second, you must receive Christ by doing three things: (1) Recognize and admit your sins. The Bible says, "For all have sinned, and come short of the glory of God" (Romans 3:23). (2) Repent of your sins. Jesus said, "No, I tell you; but unless you repent, you will all likewise perish (die)" (Luke 13:3). Repentance means you recognize your sins; you admit your life is headed in the wrong direction, and now you must be willing to turn your back on sin and turn your heart to Christ. (3) Receive Jesus Christ as your personal Lord and Savior. Commit your heart to Him by faith—in childlike faith; showing the good qualities that children have, such as trusting people, being honest and enthusiastic, expressing a childlike innocence or quality.

> "The Lord is not slack concerning His promise, as some men count slackness; but is longsuffering toward us, not willing that any should perish, but that all should come to repentance" (2 Peter 3:9).

That word "men" in the Greek is generic; it means "men and women." Therefore, if you have never recognized and repented of your sins (changed your carnal ways). If you've never had a relationship with God. Or perhaps, you are backslidden or away from God or you've wandered. The Bible says, "I will heal your backsliding, I will love them freely: for My anger is turned away from him" (Hosea 14:4). You can come home to your heavenly Father today, and He will love you, and forgive you, and cleanse you, and strengthen you to be what He's called you to be.

It isn't by accident that you are reading this book. I believe the Lord by His leading and His mercy brought us together. And so, I want to ask you to pray the prayer of salvation—also called the prayer of faith and sometimes called the sinner's prayer—to make peace with God. Just, with a sincere heart, pray the prayer of salvation out loud in childlike faith and make a commitment right now.

Why out loud? Because Christ did everything publicly.

"For whosoever shall be ashamed of Me and of My words, of him shall the Son of Man be ashamed, when He comes in the glory of His Father with His holy angels" (Luke 9:26; also in Mark 8:38).

And after you've done that, go to our Publisher Website at https://www.RidgePublishingGroup.com, and click on "Subscribe" to receive our monthly **Guardians of Biblical Truth New Beginnings Newsletter** sent directly to your inbox. Also, on our website, you will find the prequel to this book, Passion for Christ: New Beginnings, available for free in PDF format when you subscribe. The e-book and print book versions are both available for purchase at Amazon.com and other retailers. Then, follow us on our Amazon Author Central page and learn more about next steps in your walk with God as we upload more Bible-based books. Why? Because this isn't the end of what God's going to do in your life, just the beginning.

"Go therefore and make disciples of all nations, baptizing them in the name of the Father and of the Son and of the Holy Spirit, teaching them to observe all that I have commanded you. And behold, I am with you always, to the end of the age" (Matthew 28:19-20).

With a sincere heart, just pray this, out loud:

"Heavenly Father, today as I was reading the Bible, you were speaking to me. I want to be right with God. I recognize my sins and I ask for forgiveness. I believe Jesus Christ is your Son. I believe that He died on the cross as payment for sin and rose again as the hope of the world. And I recognize that Jesus is the only salvation and the only Savior available.

In childlike faith, I trust in the Lord Jesus from this day forward. I repent of my sins, and I trust in the blood that was shed on the cross for the forgiveness of my sins. Cleanse me; my mind, my body, and my spirit. Come into my heart. And I vow this day, I will live for you all the days of my life. Guide my life and help me to do your will. Fill me with the Holy Spirit and give me the power to be what you want me to be. Be my Lord and Savior.

According to the Bible which cannot lie, all who call upon the name of the Lord, shall be saved. Today, I'm saved. I'm forgiven. I'm delivered. I'm healed. The curse of sin and sickness and lack in my life are now broken. And I have become the righteousness of God through Jesus Christ. And I'll never be the same. I pray this in Jesus Christ's precious name. Amen."

The Bible said either your Father is God, or your father is the devil. And the Bible said that the power of sin and Satan comes to steal, and to kill, and to destroy. But Jesus said:

"The thief comes not, but for to steal, and to kill, and to destroy; I come that they might have life, and that they might have it more abundantly" (John 10:10).

Jesus is the master of life. And if you want to walk in the life of forgiveness and have that relationship with God the Father, you can begin that today. All you have to do is pray the prayer of salvation to make peace with God—in doing so, you become a born again Christian.

"Therefore if any man be in Christ, he is a new creature: old things are passed away; behold, all things become new" (2 Corinthians 5:17).

"Total Surrender: My Story and Your Blueprint for a Meaningful Life" is not just an autobiography about my call with God. It is a clarion call (a call to something that is hard to ignore). It is a wakeup call to all of humanity to choose God before it's too late; and get prepared for the second coming of Jesus Christ, our Lord and Savior—time is near, He is knocking at the door:

> "Behold, I stand at the door and knock. If anyone hears My voice and opens the door, I will come in to him and eat with him, and he with Me" (Revelation 3:20).

When you know God and understand the wisdom of the Bible, it will change you! This is our calling—our true purpose in life. Let the Lord into your life; He has a plan . . . when you do that, amazing things start to happen: You'll become passionate about God. You'll begin to crave to think and speak in line with Jesus' ways. You'll start to see yourself the way Christ sees you. You'll habitually tune into the Holy Spirit, who lives within those in Christ, to check for a sense of peace in your choices. And then miracles begin to happen . . .

DRENCHED IN FAITH

CHAPTER ONE

The Baptismal Prelude: Historical Roots and Ritual Significance

"Therefore we have been buried with him by baptism into death, so that, just as Christ was raised from the dead by the glory of the Father, so we too might walk in newness of life." —ROMANS 6:4 NRSV

Imagine yourself standing on the banks of the Jordan River, where the waters flow with a timeless current that carries the echoes of ages past. Here, the river is not just a river; it's a conduit for history, a vessel for faith, and the stage for a sacred rite that has shaped the lives of countless believers. Welcome to Chapter 1 of "Drenched in Faith: The Transformative Act of Water Baptism."

In this chapter, we embark on a journey that traverses the annals of history, tracing the origins and evolution of water baptism. It's a journey that will take us back to ancient civilizations, where water was revered for its cleansing properties, and forward to contemporary times, where the ritual continues to hold profound significance. As we navigate the meandering waters of this narrative, we will unearth the historical roots, delve into the symbolism, and uncover the theological depths that make baptism a transformative act within the Christian tradition.

Our expedition begins by casting a historical net wide enough to capture the diverse influences that have contributed to the development of water baptism. From the sacred rivers of antiquity, where purification rites were performed, to the emergence of Christian sacraments, we will explore the rich tapestry of traditions that have woven their threads into the fabric of baptism.

The journey will then guide us through the corridors of the New Testament, where we encounter pivotal moments such as the baptism of Jesus by John the Baptist and the Great Commission, in which Christ himself entrusted his disciples with the task of baptizing new believers. Through the scriptures, we will unlock the scriptural foundations that underpin this sacred act, illuminating its significance within the Christian faith.

But our exploration doesn't stop at the water's edge; it extends into the theological depths of baptism. We will unpack the symbolism that infuses the ritual, where water signifies cleansing, rebirth, and spiritual transformation. We will delve into the communal aspects of baptism, highlighting how it marks one's entry into the family of believers and serves as a declaration of faith. We will explore how baptism is seen as a means of forgiveness, a washing away of sins, and a tangible expression of God's grace.

As we navigate this comprehensive examination of water baptism, prepare to be immersed not only in the depths of history but also in the transformative power of faith. This chapter invites you to journey through time and tradition, to understand the origins, symbolism, and significance of this sacred rite, and to witness how it continues to shape and transform the lives of those who dare to step into its sacred waters.

So, let the river of history and faith carry you forward as we dive into "The Baptismal Prelude."

Historical Origins of Baptism

Close your eyes and imagine standing on the banks of the Jordan River, where the waters have flowed through history, witnessing countless transformations. This chapter takes you on a captivating journey to uncover the historical origins of water baptism, a sacred ritual that finds its roots in ancient traditions and bears a rich significance within the Christian faith.

The flowing waters of history often mirror the spiritual currents, and in the sacred texts of the Bible, water holds a central place. In Genesis 1:2, we read how "the Spirit of God was hovering over the waters," hinting at the creative and transformative power of water from the very beginning. Water's purifying qualities are exemplified in Exodus 30:20–21, where it is used for ritual cleansing.

Our exploration begins with the historical tapestry of baptism, a practice that transcends time and culture. Long before it became a Christian sacrament, water played a central role in purification rituals across various cultures and religions. The Jewish practice of mikveh, a ritual immersion in a pool of water, was a precursor to Christian baptism, and its roots stretch back into the annals of Jewish history.

The Old Testament provides glimpses into the significance of water in purification. In 2 Kings 5:1–14, we encounter the story of Naaman, a Syrian general who was healed of leprosy after being instructed by the prophet Elisha to dip himself seven times in the Jordan River. His cleansing is a vivid illustration of water's transformative power.

As we journey through history, we discover how early Christians embraced the act of baptism. Jesus himself was baptized by John the Baptist in the Jordan River, a momentous event symbolizing his identification with humanity and the initiation of his earthly ministry (Matthew 3:13–17). Following this, Jesus issued the Great Commission, instructing his disciples to baptize new believers in the name of the Father, Son, and Holy Spirit (Matthew 28:19–20).

These passages illustrate the pivotal role of water baptism in the life of Jesus and the early Christian community. They underscore the divine endorsement of this transformative ritual.

Our journey through history brings us face-to-face with the diverse influences and scriptural underpinnings of water baptism. As we stand on the banks of the Jordan River, we can feel the weight of history and faith intertwining like the currents of this sacred waterway.

In the Book of Acts, we find accounts of early Christian baptisms that provide a glimpse into the practice's significance. Acts 8 recounts Philip's encounter with the Ethiopian eunuch, who, after hearing the Gospel, requested to be baptized as they came across a body of water (Acts 8:36–39). This episode highlights the immediacy and eagerness with which new believers embraced baptism.

As we explore the historical narrative further, we encounter the writings of early Church Fathers who reflected on baptism. Figures like Augustine and Justin Martyr left behind theological treatises that deepen our understanding of this transformative ritual. Their insights reveal how baptism was seen as a spiritual birth, a cleansing from sin, and a means of receiving the Holy Spirit's indwelling presence.

In Romans 6:3–4, the apostle Paul poignantly captures the symbolism of baptism: "Do you not know that all of us who have been baptized into Christ Jesus were baptized into his death? We were buried therefore with him by baptism into death, in order that, just as Christ was raised from the dead by the glory of the Father, we too might walk in newness of life." These words offer profound insight into the spiritual rebirth that baptism symbolizes.

As we journey through history and scripture, we begin to unravel the layers of meaning behind water baptism. It emerges as a powerful symbol of cleansing, rebirth, and spiritual transformation, carrying deep roots in both the history of faith and the pages of sacred texts.

Our exploration continues into the symbolism and ritual significance of baptism in the following sections of this chapter, shedding light on the transformative power it holds within the Christian tradition and the lives of believers. The waters of the Jordan River may have flowed through history, but it is the waters of baptism that continue to flow through the hearts and souls of those who undergo this sacred rite, ushering them into a new and profound spiritual journey.

———————

Rivers of Renewal: Aurora's Journey Through the History and Impact of Baptism

In the serene town of Elmsworth, a place where tradition and modernity intertwined like the branches of its ancient oaks, there lived a woman named Aurora. She was a renowned historian and a professor who had spent decades studying the cultural and spiritual practices of ancient and modern civilizations. Her passion was not just to teach about history, but to make it come alive for her students and her community. Aurora's fascination with the transformative power of water in various rituals across cultures had led her to explore deeply the Christian sacrament of baptism. Inspired by her studies and the impact of her faith on her own life, she decided to create an engaging exhibition at the local museum titled "Waters of Life: The Journey of Baptism Through the Ages."

The exhibit aimed to showcase the historical origins of water baptism, tracing its roots from ancient purification rituals to its integral role in Christian traditions. Aurora used replicas of ancient artifacts, interactive multimedia presentations, and excerpts from sacred texts to illustrate the journey. One section featured a large, tranquil pool designed to replicate the Jordan River, surrounded by reeds and stones, where visitors could pause and reflect.

The highlight of the exhibition was a series of personal stories from community members who had undergone baptism, each sharing their unique experiences and the impact of this rite on their lives. These stories were displayed alongside ancient scriptures and teachings from early Church Fathers, creating a bridge between past and present.

One poignant story was that of Michael, a local firefighter who had turned to faith during a time of personal crisis. His baptism in the nearby river was a public declaration of his new path in life, symbolizing a cleansing from past regrets and a commitment to live with purpose and faith. His story resonated deeply with visitors, who saw in his experience a modern reflection of the ancient texts and rituals displayed throughout the exhibit.

Aurora also organized guided tours, where she shared insights into how the act of baptism has been viewed over centuries—a symbol of purification, a rite of passage, and a profound declaration of faith. She explained how, in the early Christian community, baptism was not only about personal transformation but also about creating a sense of belonging and unity among believers.

As the exhibition gained popularity, Aurora noticed how it became a place of contemplation and conversation among visitors of all ages and backgrounds. Schools started organizing trips to the museum, and local church groups visited to connect more deeply with their faith's historical roots.

Through "Waters of Life," Aurora not only educated her community about the historical and spiritual significance of baptism but also created a space where people could reflect on their own life journeys. The exhibit reminded them that, much like the waters of the Jordan have seen countless transformations over the ages, each individual has the potential for renewal and change.

Aurora's story, like the water itself, became a source of inspiration, showing that understanding our past can guide us in our present and shape our future. Her dedication to bringing history to life demonstrated the value of learning from our traditions to forge deeper connections with our beliefs and with each other.

———————

As we journey deeper into the heart of water baptism, we find ourselves at the confluence of history and faith. The waters that once flowed through ancient purification rituals and biblical narratives now converge in the Christian sacrament of baptism, a transformative act of profound significance.

In the Gospel of John, Jesus tells Nicodemus, "Truly, truly, I say to you, unless one is born of water and the Spirit, he cannot enter the kingdom of God" (John 3:5). These words underscore the vital role of baptism as a spiritual rebirth, a gateway to the Kingdom of God.

The symbolism of baptism is a rich tapestry of meaning. Immersion in water signifies a cleansing from sin, a burial of the old self, and a rising to newness of life. The act mirrors the death, burial, and resurrection of Jesus, making it a powerful declaration of faith.

In Colossians 2:12, Paul writes, "having been buried with him in baptism, in which you were also raised with him through faith in the powerful working of God, who raised him from the dead." This verse encapsulates the transformative essence of baptism, aligning believers with the life-altering power of Christ's resurrection.

But the significance of baptism doesn't stop at the water's edge. It extends to the community of believers. Baptism marks one's initiation into the body of Christ, signifying unity with fellow believers and a commitment to walk in faith together.

In 1 Corinthians 12:13, Paul beautifully captures this communal aspect, declaring, "For in one Spirit we were all baptized into one body—Jews or Greeks, slaves or free—and all were made to drink of one Spirit." Baptism is not merely an individual experience; it connects believers to a larger spiritual family.

As we journey through history and scripture, the significance of water baptism becomes increasingly profound. It is a sacred act that bridges the past and present, uniting believers with ancient traditions and biblical narratives. It is a transformative rite that cleanses, renews, and connects individuals to the heart of the Christian faith.

In the chapters that follow, we will delve even deeper into the transformative power of water baptism. We will explore its contemporary relevance and the personal stories of individuals whose lives have been forever changed by the waters of faith. As we navigate this spiritual journey, we'll witness how this age-old ritual continues to shape and transform the lives of those who dare to step into its sacred stream.

Baptism in the Christian Tradition

Our journey through the pages of history now leads us to a pivotal crossroad—the role of water baptism within the Christian tradition. Here, we find the ancient meeting the eternal, where the waters of baptism become a timeless symbol of faith, cleansing, and rebirth.

In the New Testament, we encounter the narrative of baptism unfolding with a profound spiritual resonance that echoes through the ages. Picture yourself standing on the banks of the Jordan River alongside John the Baptist, who proclaimed in Matthew 3:11, "I baptize you with water for repentance, but he who is coming after me is mightier than I, whose sandals I am not worthy to carry. He will baptize you with the Holy Spirit and fire." John's words heralded the arrival of Jesus, the one who would transform the ritual of baptism into a profound sacrament.

Water baptism, as practiced by Christians today, finds its roots in these early moments of Christian history. It signifies far more than a mere immersion in water; it signifies a transformative journey, a sacred initiation into the Christian faith.

In Acts 22:16, we see the apostle Paul's own baptism narrative as he recounted, "And now why do you wait? Rise and be baptized and wash away your sins, calling on His name." Paul's experience on the road to Damascus encapsulates the profound change and purification that baptism represents.

The Great Commission, as found in Matthew 28:19–20, stands as a cornerstone of Christian belief and practice. Here, Jesus instructs his disciples, saying, "Go therefore and make disciples of all nations, baptizing them in the name of the Father and of the Son and of the Holy Spirit, teaching them to observe all that I have commanded you." These words reverberate through time, emphasizing the significance of baptism as a means of initiating new believers into the Christian community and faith.

In Acts 8:12, we encounter the early Christian practice of baptism as part of the conversion process: "But when they believed Philip as he preached good news about the kingdom of God and the name of Jesus Christ, they were baptized, both men and women." This verse showcases the seamless connection between faith and baptism, highlighting how baptism marked the commitment of new believers.

The waters of baptism, from the Jordan River's banks to the baptistries of modern churches, continue to echo with these ancient words and practices. The act of water baptism serves as a tangible reminder of the transformative power of faith, a connection to the rich history of Christian belief, and an entry point into the community of believers.

In the following section of this chapter, we will delve deeper into the symbolism and theological significance of water baptism, unveiling the layers of meaning that make it a cornerstone of the Christian faith. As we explore further, we'll witness how this sacred act transcends time and culture, offering believers a profound encounter with the divine.

Waters of Legacy: Lucy's Journey Through Baptismal Heritage

Lucy Anderson had always felt a disconnect from her spiritual roots, despite growing up in a family where church attendance was as regular as Sunday dinner. It wasn't until her grandmother passed away that Lucy found herself sorting through old family albums and stumbled upon a photograph that would change her perspective entirely—a black and white image of her great-grandfather being baptized in the Jordan River.

Curiosity piqued, Lucy embarked on a journey to explore the significance of water baptism within her family and the broader Christian tradition. She learned that her great-grandfather had made a pilgrimage to the Holy Land in the early 20th century, a journey that culminated in his baptism in the very waters where John the Baptist once baptized Jesus. This act was not just a personal milestone; it was a declaration of faith that deeply influenced the subsequent generations.

Driven by a newfound understanding and a desire to experience this transformative ritual herself, Lucy decided to participate in a baptism ceremony at her local church. Standing in the baptismal pool, she recalled the words of Matthew 3:11, spoken by John the Baptist, echoing the profound spiritual resonance of the rite—how it symbolized cleansing, rebirth, and a personal connection to the eternal journey of faith practiced by Christians throughout the ages.

As the pastor recited the Great Commission, Lucy felt a wave of emotions. Immersed in the water, she felt a link not just to her great-grandfather but to the multitude of believers who had embraced this sacred act over millennia. It was a powerful moment of unity and continuity, a tangible connection to her heritage and a personal commitment to live out the teachings of Jesus.

Lucy's baptism marked a pivotal moment in her life. It was not just about following in her great-grandfather's footsteps or observing a religious formality. It became a personal anchor, a spiritual awakening that redefined her faith and her place within the community of believers. Her story became a testimony shared within her church, inspiring others to explore the depths of their faith and the historical roots that connect them to generations past.

In this act of baptism, Lucy found more than just spiritual renewal; she rediscovered a family legacy of faith that bridged generations, cultures, and geographies, uniting them in the shared waters of belief and belonging.

====

Symbolism and Ritual Significance

As we dive deeper into the profound waters of baptism, we encounter a rich tapestry of symbolism that adds layers of meaning to this sacred rite. Water, in particular, takes on a role of paramount significance, signifying cleansing, rebirth, and spiritual transformation.

Water, from the earliest pages of the Bible, has held a unique place in the narrative of faith. Again, in Genesis 1:2, we read how "the Spirit of God was hovering over the waters," underscoring the creative and transformative power of water from the very beginning. Water's cleansing qualities are exemplified in Exodus 30:20–21, where it is used for ritual purification.

In the act of baptism, water serves as a powerful symbol of cleansing—a cleansing not just of the body but of the soul. It is the moment when a person sheds the weight of their past, their transgressions, and emerges from the waters, reborn and renewed.

In Acts 22:16, we see the apostle Paul's own baptism narrative as he recounted, "And now why do you wait? Rise and be baptized and wash away your sins, calling on his name." This verse encapsulates the profound change and purification that baptism represents.

Furthermore, water baptism is a symbolic reenactment of Christ's own death, burial, and resurrection. When a believer is immersed in the water, it symbolizes their identification with the crucifixion and burial of Jesus, and when they rise from the water, it signifies their sharing in the resurrection life of Christ.

In Romans 6:3–4, the apostle Paul beautifully captures the symbolism of baptism: "Do you not know that all of us who have been baptized into Christ Jesus were baptized into his death? We were buried therefore with him by baptism into death, in order that, just as Christ was raised from the dead by the glory of the Father, we too might walk in newness of life." These words offer profound insight into the spiritual rebirth that baptism symbolizes.

But baptism is not merely a ritual; it carries profound theological significance. It marks one's entry into the faith, signifying a commitment to follow Christ and embrace the Christian community. It is a public declaration of one's identity as a follower of Jesus.

In Galatians 3:26–27, Paul writes, "for in Christ Jesus you are all sons of God, through faith. For as many of you as were baptized into Christ have put on Christ." This passage underscores the transformative nature of baptism and the profound identity shift that occurs.

Baptism is also seen as a means of forgiveness, a spiritual washing away of sins. It signifies a fresh start, a clean slate, and a reconciliation with God.

In Acts 2:38, after Peter's sermon on the Day of Pentecost, he declares, "Repent and be baptized, every one of you, in the name of Jesus Christ for the forgiveness of your sins." Here, we witness the close connection between baptism and the forgiveness of sins.

As we navigate the symbolism and theological significance of water baptism, we'll uncover how it serves as a bridge between the spiritual and the physical, the ancient and the contemporary. In the chapters that follow, we will witness how this profound ritual continues to shape and transform the lives of those who dare to step into its sacred waters.

A New Beginning: Penelope's Embrace of Water's Grace

Penelope, a 28-year-old graphic designer from a bustling city, found herself at a crossroads, weighed down by her past mistakes and a life that seemed to spiral beyond her control. Despite her success in the creative industry, a sense of fulfillment eluded her, and the void grew larger with each passing day.

Her journey to transformation began unexpectedly during a visit to her hometown for a family reunion, where she encountered her old youth pastor, Mrs. Thompson. Over coffee, Penelope shared her feelings of disconnection and loss. Mrs. Thompson listened intently, her eyes reflecting a deep understanding. As they spoke, she gently introduced the topic of spiritual renewal and the powerful symbolism of water baptism, explaining its significance in shedding past burdens and embracing a new identity in faith.

Intrigued and somewhat desperate for a change, Penelope agreed to attend a service at Mrs. Thompson's church the following Sunday. As she listened to the sermon about the transformative power of baptism, citing Acts 22:16, where Paul speaks of rising and washing away sins through baptism, something stirred within her. The words resonated, touching a deep, unacknowledged yearning for renewal.

The next week, Penelope stood on the banks of the nearby river where the church conducted its baptisms. The water flowed gently, reflecting the morning light. Wrapped in a white robe, she stepped into the river, her heart pounding with a mix of nerves and excitement. The pastor recited Romans 6:3–4, reminding her that in baptism, she was participating in Jesus' death and resurrection, symbolically burying her old self and rising to walk anew in life's fullness.

As she was submerged, the cool water enveloped her, muffling the sounds of the world above. In those brief moments under the water, Penelope felt a release, as if the current was carrying away her past failures and pains. Emerging from the river, she gasped for air, feeling as though she could breathe for the first time in years. Her eyes gleamed with unshed tears, not of sorrow, but of joy and relief. She felt reborn, cleansed, and profoundly connected to a community that cheered her on from the riverbank.

Penelope's baptism marked a significant turning point in her life. She embraced her new path with vigor, integrating her faith into her daily living and work. Her relationships improved, imbued with the love and forgiveness she had come to know. The symbolism of water, as a source of life and purity, became a central theme in her art, influencing her designs in ways she had never imagined.

Months later, Penelope returned to the same riverbank, this time to witness others take their steps into the waters of baptism. She stood among the crowd, her heart full, as she realized how much had changed since her own baptism. Each candidate's rise from the water was a reminder of her own journey through water's grace—a journey of forgiveness, rebirth, and endless new beginnings.

Conclusion

As we stand on the shores of history, having navigated the depths of water baptism's historical roots, symbolism, and theological significance, we find ourselves at a crossroads where the past and the present converge, where ancient traditions and contemporary faith intertwine.

In this chapter, we have uncovered the rich tapestry of influences that have shaped water baptism-from the purifying waters of ancient civilizations to the sacred mikveh baths of Judaism. We've traced the journey through the New

Testament, witnessing the baptism of Jesus, the Great Commission, and the early Christian writings that illuminate the transformative power of this sacred rite.

But our exploration goes beyond the pages of history and scripture; it delves into the very essence of what baptism signifies. We've immersed ourselves in the symbolism of water, where it cleanses, purifies, and signifies a spiritual rebirth. We've plunged into the depths of death and resurrection, where baptism becomes a profound identification with Christ's redemptive work.

As we conclude this chapter, let us not forget that the waters of baptism, once stirred by John the Baptist in the Jordan, continue to ripple through time, touching the lives of countless individuals who dare to step into its sacred stream. It is not merely a historical relic but a living, breathing practice that bridges the past with the present, offering believers a tangible connection to their faith's roots.

In the chapters that follow, we will dive even deeper into the transformative power of water baptism. We will witness personal stories of individuals whose lives have been forever changed by the waters of faith. We will explore the contemporary relevance of this age-old ritual and its enduring impact on the Christian community.

THE BAPTISMAL PRELUDE

So, as we move forward in our journey, let the echoes of history and faith continue to guide us. For within the waters of baptism, we find not only a connection to the past but an invitation to a renewed and transformed future—a future drenched in faith.

CHAPTER TWO

Cleansing Waters: Understanding Baptism's Symbolism

"Therefore, if anyone is in Christ, the new creation has come: The old has gone, the new is here!" —2 CORINTHIANS 5:17 NIV

In the heart of our journey into the transformative act of water baptism, we find ourselves drawn to the very essence of this sacred rite—the profound symbolism it carries. Chapter 2, "Cleansing Waters: Understanding Baptism's Symbolism," invites us to wade into deeper waters, where the physical act of immersion gives way to a rich tapestry of spiritual meaning.

Imagine standing at the threshold of a river, the waters shimmering with centuries of wisdom and revelation. As we step into these cleansing waters, we embark on a journey that transcends the limits of words. We explore the age-old belief in water's purifying power, both in the context of diverse cultures and the sacred pages of scripture.

But our journey doesn't stop at the surface; it delves into the depths of the soul, where baptism becomes a spiritual rebirth. We'll uncover the profound connection between immersion in water and the washing away of sins, the emergence of a new, redeemed self. Through personal stories and testimonials, we'll witness the tangible transformation that occurs in the sacred embrace of baptismal waters.

As we navigate further, we'll dive into the New Testament's baptismal imagery, where the apostles paint vivid portraits of this sacred ritual. Passages like Romans 6:3–4 and Galatians 3:27 will be our guides, revealing how baptism is not just an external act but a participation in the very life, death, and resurrection of Christ.

So, as we journey through the symbolism of baptism, prepare to be immersed in a narrative that goes beyond ritual— it delves into the profound and eternal truths that these cleansing waters represent. It's an exploration of faith, renewal, and transformation, where water is not just an element but a vessel that carries the promise of redemption. Welcome to "Cleansing Waters," where the symbolism of baptism becomes a river of revelation, inviting us to step in and be forever changed.

Water as Purification

In the heart of our exploration of baptism's profound symbolism, we find ourselves drawn to the ancient and universal significance of water as a purifying element. As we dip our toes into this topic, we embark on a journey that transcends time, cultures, and faiths, uncovering the spiritual depth that water has carried through history.

Water's cleansing power is a concept deeply ingrained in the human experience, and it extends far beyond the pages of the Bible. From the banks of the Ganges in India, where millions seek spiritual purification, to the rituals of ancient civilizations that used water for physical and spiritual cleansing, we discover a common thread that links diverse traditions. It is a thread woven with the understanding that water possesses a unique ability to wash away impurities and bring renewal.

In the biblical narrative, we encounter numerous instances where water is used as a symbol of cleansing. One of the most poignant is found in Psalm 51:7, where King David implores, "Purge me with hyssop, and I shall be clean; wash me, and I shall be whiter than snow." These words evoke the idea of water's transformative power, not only in purifying the body but also in cleansing the soul.

As we draw parallels between these ancient practices and the symbolism of water in Christian baptism, we see how the act of immersion in water signifies more than a mere physical cleansing. It becomes a spiritual purification, a shedding of the old self, and a rising of the new. In the waters of baptism, believers are invited to partake in a ritual that transcends cultural and historical boundaries, embracing the universal truth that water symbolizes renewal and transformation.

Our journey into the symbolism of water as purification goes beyond the surface, delving into the depths of faith and spirituality. It reminds us that water is not just a substance but a vessel, a sacred conduit that carries the promise of cleansing and renewal. It is a reminder that in the act of baptism, we are not only washed with water but immersed in a profound symbol of God's grace, forgiveness, and the opportunity for a fresh start.

As we continue our exploration of baptism's symbolism, we will delve deeper into the spiritual rebirth that it represents. We will uncover personal stories of individuals who have found new life through these cleansing waters, offering living testimony to the enduring power of this age-old ritual.

***

The Renewal of Leah: A Journey Through Water's Purifying Grace

Leah, a 38-year-old teacher from the bustling city of Chicago, found herself at a crossroads. Despite her successful career and a loving family, there was a palpable emptiness—a yearning for a spiritual cleansing that the complexities of daily life could not wash away. Leah's journey towards spiritual purification began unexpectedly, during a visit to a local church, where she witnessed a baptism.

As the water washed over the individual being baptized, Leah felt a profound connection to the act. The concept of water as a purifying agent, which she had read about in various cultures and religious practices, resonated deeply with her. She too recalled reading about the sacred Ganges in India, where water symbolizes a direct pathway to purification, and the ancient Roman baths, which were not only for physical cleanliness but spiritual renewal.

Motivated by these reflections and moved by the ceremony, Leah decided to partake in the baptismal rite herself. Her decision was not merely about following a tradition but seeking a personal transformation—a desire to cleanse her past burdens and start anew. The day of her baptism, she stood by the edge of the baptismal pool, her heart pounding with a mixture of nervousness and excitement.

As she was immersed in the water, Leah experienced a moment of overwhelming clarity. The coolness enveloped her, and for a moment, it was as though time stood still. She emerged feeling a weight had been lifted. The words from Psalm 51:7 echoed in her mind, "Purge me with hyssop, and I shall be clean; wash me, and I shall be whiter than snow." This verse took on a new, profound meaning for her—it wasn't just about physical cleanliness but a deeper, spiritual renewal.

This baptism marked a significant turn in Leah's life. She found herself more engaged with her community, more patient with her students, and more present with her family. The act of baptism, as a symbol of purification, had transformed her, renewing her spirit and perspective on life.

Leah's story became a testament to the power of baptism's symbolism within her community. She shared her experience openly, discussing how the act was more than a ritual—it was a gateway to a new way of being, a purification not just of the body, but of the soul.

Her journey serves as a reminder that across cultures and ages, water remains a powerful symbol of renewal and purity. For Leah, and for many others, baptism is not the end but the beginning of a path marked by continuous spiritual growth and transformation. As her story spreads, it inspires others to explore the profound impact of this ancient ritual, encouraging them to experience the rejuvenating powers of these cleansing waters.

———

Our journey into the profound symbolism of water baptism carries us further into the heart of this sacred rite, where water, with its cleansing properties, serves as a bridge between diverse cultures, faiths, and ages.

Water's purifying essence is an age-old belief that has resonated across the annals of history and across the globe. From the holy Ganges River in India, where millions seek spiritual purification, to the ancient baths of Rome, where physical and spiritual cleansing were intertwined, water has consistently held the power to wash away impurities, both external and internal.

In the scriptures, this concept of water's transformative power is eloquently expressed. In the book of Ezekiel, God speaks of cleansing His people with water, saying, "I will sprinkle clean water on you, and you shall be clean from all your uncleannesses" (Ezekiel 36:25). This profound imagery illustrates the spiritual cleansing that water signifies in the context of faith.

As we weave together these historical and scriptural threads, we see the parallels between these ancient practices and the symbolism of water in Christian baptism. The act of being immersed in water goes beyond mere ritual; it becomes a profound spiritual purification. It signifies not only the washing away of sins but the emergence of a new, redeemed self.

In Christian baptism, we witness the convergence of diverse traditions and cultures, where the universal truth that water symbolizes renewal and transformation takes center stage. The waters of baptism are not stagnant; they flow through history, inviting believers to step into their current and experience the cleansing, purifying, and renewing power of faith.

This exploration of water's role as a symbol of purification serves as a reminder that baptism is not merely an external act but a deeply spiritual one. It invites us to recognize that in the act of immersion, we are not only cleansed physically but immersed in the profound symbol of God's grace and forgiveness. Baptism is the gateway to a fresh start, a spiritual renewal, and a transformative journey.

As we journey deeper into the symbolism of baptism, we will uncover even more layers of meaning and significance. We will continue to explore how the waters of faith have the power to cleanse not only the body but also the soul. We will bear witness to the stories of individuals who have experienced this cleansing firsthand, testifying to the enduring power of baptism's symbolism.

———

Journey of Renewal: Mei's Embrace of Spiritual Waters

Mei, a 45-year-old art curator from San Francisco, had always been drawn to the transformative power of art and its ability to convey deep spiritual truths. However, her connection to her own spiritual path felt unclear and stagnant. It wasn't until a trip to Varanasi, India, that she encountered the profound symbolism of water in a way that would forever change her perspective.

Standing on the bustling ghats of the Ganges, Mei watched as countless pilgrims entered the river. They came with the belief that the sacred waters would cleanse them of their sins and offer renewal. This powerful scene struck a chord with

Mei, awakening a yearning for her own spiritual purification and renewal.

Upon returning home, Mei's experience in India lingered in her mind, leading her to explore the spiritual significance of water in different cultures and religions. Her research brought her to the Christian practice of baptism, a ritual she had seen but never deeply understood. The more she learned, the more she felt drawn to the symbolic act of being immersed in water, not just for physical cleansing, but for a profound spiritual rebirth.

Inspired by her journey and the scripture from Ezekiel 36:25, "I will sprinkle clean water on you, and you shall be clean from all your uncleannesses," Mei decided to undergo baptism. She approached a local church, where she shared her story and her desire to experience baptism not just as a ritual, but as a personal transformation.

The day of her baptism was a poignant moment for Mei. As she was immersed in the water, she felt as though the weight of her past doubts and uncertainties were being washed away. Emerging from the water, Mei experienced what many describe as a rebirth; she felt renewed, with a newfound clarity and connection to her spiritual path.

Mei's transformation had a ripple effect in her life. She began integrating her spiritual beliefs into her work, curating exhibits that explored the intersection of art, spirituality, and the symbolism of water. She also became more active in her community, sharing her journey and the impact of her baptism with others who were seeking spiritual guidance.

Her story became a testament to the power of baptism's symbolism—a narrative of renewal that transcended cultural and religious boundaries. Mei's experience highlighted how the act of baptism, rooted in ancient traditions, continues to offer individuals a profound experience of cleansing, renewal, and transformation.

As Mei continued to explore and grow in her faith, she became a beacon of hope and inspiration, a living testimony to the enduring power of water's purifying essence in baptism. Her journey, from the banks of the Ganges to the baptismal waters of her local church, serves as a vivid illustration of how deeply spiritual symbols like water can touch and transform lives.

———

As we navigate the depths of water baptism's symbolism, we find ourselves on a profound journey through history, spirituality, and faith. Our exploration of water's role as a purifying element unveils a tapestry woven with threads of universal significance.

Across cultures and religions, water has consistently been recognized as a purifying force—a sacred conduit that washes away impurities and brings forth renewal. From the ancient baths of Greece to the ritual ablutions in Islam, water has served as a symbol of spiritual cleansing. It is a concept that transcends borders and bridges the gap between diverse traditions.

Within the pages of the Bible, we encounter vivid imagery that underscores the spiritual significance of water. In the Old Testament, the prophet Isaiah declares, "Come now, let us settle the matter. Though your sins are like scarlet, they shall be as white as snow; though they are red as crimson, they shall be like wool" (Isaiah 1:18). This imagery of sins being washed away like scarlet stains in the snow beautifully encapsulates the concept of water as a purifier.

In the context of Christian baptism, we witness the convergence of these ancient beliefs and the timeless truth of faith. The act of immersion in water represents not just a physical cleansing but a spiritual purification—a shedding of the old self and the emergence of a new creation. In the waters of baptism, believers are invited to experience a cleansing that goes beyond the skin and reaches deep into the soul.

In Christian baptism, water becomes a profound symbol of God's grace, forgiveness, and the promise of a fresh start. It is a powerful reminder that, in the act of immersion, we are not only cleansed from sin but also initiated into a spiritual journey of renewal and transformation.

As we continue to explore the symbolism of water as purification, we will delve even deeper into the spiritual rebirth that baptism represents. We will witness personal testimonies of individuals whose lives have been forever changed by these cleansing waters, offering living proof of the enduring power of this ancient yet timeless ritual.

Our journey into the symbolism of baptism is far from over. In the chapters that follow, we will unravel more layers of significance and meaning, exploring the spiritual depths that continue to make baptism a transformative act for those who step into its cleansing waters.

Baptism as a Spiritual Rebirth

In our exploration of baptism's profound symbolism, we now embark on a voyage that delves into the very heart of this sacred rite—its role as a catalyst for spiritual rebirth. Beyond the waters of physical cleansing, we find the transformative currents of faith that wash away the stains of sin and unveil a new, redeemed self. |

The concept of spiritual rebirth is not new; it reverberates through the ages and across cultures. In the Gospel of John, Jesus himself alluded to this spiritual transformation when he said, "Truly, truly, I say to you, unless one is born again, he cannot see the kingdom of God" (John 3:3). These words resonate deeply with the essence of baptism as a rebirth—a shedding of the old and an emergence of the new.

As we explore the connection between baptism and spiritual rebirth, we uncover personal stories and testimonials of individuals who have experienced this profound transformation through the sacred waters. These narratives are like pearls of wisdom, shining with the authenticity of lived experiences, and they demonstrate the enduring power of baptism's symbolism.

Consider the story of Sarah, a woman burdened by the weight of past mistakes and regrets. Through her journey of faith, she found herself at the edge of a river, where the waters of baptism offered her a chance at renewal. As she emerged from the river, she felt a weight lifted from her shoulders, and she knew that she was a new creation in Christ.

In the act of baptism, Sarah and countless others have found not just physical cleansing but a spiritual purification that reaches deep into the soul. It is a powerful reminder that baptism is not a mere ritual; it is a profound encounter with the divine—a moment when old burdens are washed away, and the promise of a fresh start is embraced.

The stories of rebirth through baptism are as varied as the individuals themselves. Some have faced addiction and found deliverance, while others have grappled with doubt and discovered unwavering faith. These stories remind us that the transformative power of baptism transcends the boundaries of personal history and challenges. It is an invitation to all who seek spiritual renewal, a chance to leave behind the old self and step into the newness of life.

As we navigate the currents of baptism as a spiritual rebirth, we find ourselves immersed in the depths of faith and the promise of transformation. These stories are not just anecdotes; they are testimonies to the enduring truth that in the waters of baptism, we encounter the opportunity for a fresh start, a redeemed self, and a profound rebirth in the embrace of God's grace.

In the chapters that follow, we will continue to unravel the layers of baptism's symbolism, exploring how it cleanses not only the body but also the soul, and how it marks a profound spiritual journey of rebirth and transformation.

A New Dawn: The Story of Julian and His Path to Redemption

Julian, a 38-year-old former software developer from Seattle, had reached a point in his life where everything seemed to crumble around him. Struggling with a demanding career and battling an escalating addiction, Julian found himself alienated from his friends and family, and increasingly skeptical of any chance for redemption.

The turning point came during a community outreach program where Julian, feeling utterly defeated, heard a speaker talk about the concept of spiritual rebirth through baptism. The speaker quoted John 3:3, where Jesus spoke of being "born again" to see the kingdom of God. This message struck a chord with Julian, planting a seed of hope in his heart.

Motivated by this new perspective, Julian attended a local church service where he met people who had undergone transformations through their faith. Their stories of overcoming hardships through spiritual renewal inspired him to explore baptism as a pathway to cleanse his past and rejuvenate his spirit.

After several months of attending church and participating in group therapy sessions, Julian decided to be baptized. Standing at the edge of a natural lake surrounded by community members and new friends, he felt the weight of his past and his fears about the future. As he was submerged in the cool waters, Julian experienced a profound sense of release, as if the water was physically washing away his sins and the burdens of his old life.

Emerging from the water, Julian felt an overwhelming sense of peace and renewal. He described it as being given a second chance at life, where he was not just cleansed physically but spiritually reborn. The community around him cheered, welcoming him into this new phase of life with open arms.

In the weeks and months that followed, Julian's life underwent remarkable changes. He found the strength to overcome his addiction, rebuilt his relationships, and started volunteering at the same outreach program that had inspired his journey. Julian began sharing his story of rebirth with others, serving as a beacon of hope for those who felt as lost as he once had.

His transformation became a testament to the power of baptism as not only a symbol but a catalyst for profound spiritual change. Julian's story exemplified how baptism's ancient ritual could still profoundly affect modern lives, offering not just redemption but a complete renewal of spirit.

As we delve deeper into the symbolism of baptism in the subsequent chapters, stories like Julian's highlight the enduring power and relevance of this sacred act. His narrative of rebirth and redemption continues to inspire those around him, reinforcing the belief that anyone, regardless of their past, can find a new beginning and a renewed sense of purpose through the transformative waters of baptism.

Baptismal Imagery in the New Testament

In our journey through the symbolism of baptism, we now find ourselves on the hallowed ground of the New Testament, where profound imagery related to baptism springs forth like living water. These scriptures are not just words on a page; they are the brushstrokes of divine revelation, painting a vivid portrait of baptism's symbolism.

One of the most striking passages in the New Testament that delves into the symbolism of baptism is found in Romans 6:3–4. Here, the apostle Paul employs powerful metaphors to convey the essence of baptism: "Do you not know that all of us who have been baptized into Christ Jesus were baptized into his death? We were buried therefore with him by baptism into death, in order that, just as Christ was raised from the dead by the glory of the Father, we too might walk in newness of life."

These words paint a profound picture—a picture of immersion into the waters of baptism as a participation in

Christ's death and burial, and the emergence from those waters as a symbol of resurrection and new life. This metaphorical language invites us to contemplate the deeper layers of meaning within the act of baptism—it is not just a ritual but a profound identification with the life, death, and resurrection of Christ.

Another gem of baptismal imagery can be found in Galatians 3:27: "For as many of you as were baptized into Christ have put on Christ." These words offer a striking visual —the idea that in baptism, believers don a new spiritual garment, "putting on" Christ himself. It signifies a transformation at the very core of one's being, as if they have taken on the character and nature of Christ.

As we unpack these biblical metaphors, we gain a deeper understanding of the symbolism of baptism. It is not merely a ritual of cleansing but a profound act of identification and transformation. In baptism, we are buried with Christ, dying to our old selves, and raised anew, clothed with His righteousness and empowered to walk in newness of life.

The richness of these metaphors serves as a reminder that baptism is not a superficial or routine practice. It is a sacred journey—a participation in the divine drama of redemption. It is an invitation to embrace the fullness of Christ's life, death, and resurrection and to experience the profound transformation it offers.

As we continue our exploration of baptism's symbolism, we will dive even deeper into the spiritual depths that this sacred rite represents. We will uncover more layers of meaning and significance, exploring how these biblical metaphors continue to shape and inform the lives of believers who dare to step into the cleansing waters of faith.

―――――――

The Awakening of Calvin: A Journey through Water and Spirit

Calvin, a 45-year-old history teacher from Charleston, was known among his peers and students for his deep-seated skepticism about religious experiences. Despite his extensive knowledge of religious history, personal faith had always eluded him, and the rituals of Christianity, particularly baptism, seemed more historical than relevant to him.

However, everything began to shift when Calvin's beloved mother passed away. In her final days, she expressed a wish for him to explore the spiritual path she had cherished throughout her life. Respecting her last wishes, Calvin reluctantly agreed to attend a few church services, where he was particularly struck by the baptismal services he witnessed.

During one service, the pastor quoted Romans 6:3–4, explaining baptism as not just a symbol but a personal participation in the death and resurrection of Christ. This metaphor of dying to an old life and rising to a new one resonated deeply with Calvin, as he felt a profound connection between his mother's passing and his potential for a new beginning.

Motivated by this newfound perspective, Calvin decided to study baptism from a theological point of view. He delved into scriptures, particularly intrigued by Galatians 3:27, which described putting on Christ like a new garment through baptism. The imagery of wearing a new spiritual identity fascinated him, as he began to see baptism not just as a ritual of faith but as an act of profound transformation.

After months of reflection and study, Calvin chose to be baptized, seeing it as a symbolic burial of his doubts and the birth of a new faith that his mother had hoped for him. Standing before the congregation in a small church beside the very river where he used to play as a child, Calvin felt a connection to something greater than himself. As he was immersed in the cold waters, he felt as though he was leaving behind the old world of skepticism and rising to meet a new perspective filled with hope and spiritual clarity.

Emerging from the water, Calvin experienced what many before him had described—a sense of rebirth. He felt as though he had put on a new self, one that was open to the mysteries of faith. This experience profoundly affected his teachings and personal life. He began to integrate discussions of faith's transformative power into his history classes, bridging the gap between historical facts and personal faith journeys.

Calvin's baptism became a cornerstone of his life, a true spiritual rebirth that allowed him to embrace his community and faith with newfound enthusiasm. His story soon became one of the many testimonies shared in his church, inspiring others who, like him, had previously stood on the fringes of belief.

Through Calvin's journey, the profound symbolism of baptism as depicted in the New Testament scriptures transformed from ancient text to a living, breathing reality. His experience underscored the enduring power of these metaphors—not just as theological concepts but as transformative experiences that continue to impact and shape lives in deeply personal ways.

Conclusion

As we navigate the symbolic waters of baptism in the heart of Chapter 2, "Cleansing Waters: Understanding Baptism's Symbolism," we emerge not only refreshed but enlightened. The journey through the rich tapestry of purification, rebirth, and biblical imagery has revealed that baptism is no mere ritual—it is a symphony of faith, a transformative melody that resonates through the ages.

From the shores of the Ganges to the baptismal fonts of churches worldwide, we have witnessed the universal truth that water carries the promise of cleansing and renewal. In cultures and religions across the globe, water has been revered as a conduit for spiritual purification, a symbol of casting off the old and embracing the new.

The pages of the New Testament have become our guide, unveiling metaphors that deepen our understanding of baptism's symbolism. In Romans 6:3–4, we plunged into the waters of death and resurrection, where immersion represents a participation in Christ's redemptive work.

In Galatians 3:27, we discovered the image of "putting on" Christ like a new garment, embodying His character and grace. But this exploration is not confined to words on a page. It is a journey that invites us to step into the river of faith, to experience firsthand the profound transformation that occurs within the cleansing waters of baptism. Personal stories and testimonials have borne witness to lives forever changed—testimonies to the enduring power of this sacred rite.

As we conclude this chapter, we are reminded that baptism is more than a ceremony; it is an encounter with the divine, a journey of the soul, and a promise of new beginnings. The symbolism of baptism, as we have unraveled it, is a profound revelation—a truth that transcends culture, time, and tradition. It is an invitation to emerge from the waters, not only physically refreshed but spiritually reborn.

In the chapters that follow, we will delve deeper into the transformative power of baptism, exploring its contemporary relevance and the personal stories of those who have embarked on this sacred journey. But for now, let the echoes of our exploration continue to resonate within you—the symphony of purification, rebirth, and renewal. In baptism's transformative waters, we find not only a cleansing but a promise of transformation, a melody of faith that sings through the ages.

CHAPTER THREE

The Great Commission: Baptism as Christ's Command

"Therefore go and make disciples of all nations, baptizing them in the name of the Father and of the Son and of the Holy Spirit, and teaching them to obey everything I have commanded you. And surely I am with you always, to the very end of the age." —MATTHEW 28:19–20 NIV

In the sacred tapestry of Christianity, few directives bear the weight, significance, and universality of the Great Commission. It is an ancient mandate that echoes across time and space, transcending cultural boundaries and denominational lines. As we embark on the journey through Chapter 3, titled "The Great Commission: Baptism as Christ's

Command," we step onto the hallowed ground where faith transforms into action—a place where belief births discipleship.

Imagine standing on the precipice of a riverbank, the waters flowing before you like a ribbon of life. This is where the journey begins—an exploration of the very core of the Christian faith, where belief is not an end but a beginning. At the heart of this chapter lies a profound truth: baptism is not merely a ritual; it is a response—a response to a divine command, a response to the call to make disciples, to baptize, and to teach.

Our journey starts with the exploration of the biblical foundation of the Great Commission, primarily found in the words of Jesus recorded in Matthew 28:16–20. These verses, infused with divine authority, lay the groundwork for the central role that baptism plays in this sacred directive. We dive into the historical and cultural context of this command, unveiling its enduring significance within the Christian faith.

But this exploration goes beyond the pages of scripture; it extends into the waters of experience—a powerful demonstration of faith in action. Baptism is not a private affair; it is a public declaration, a testament that faith is meant to be shared and witnessed. It is a testament to the world that there is a commitment to follow Jesus—a commitment boldly proclaimed before the community of believers.

Furthermore, we will journey through the role of baptism in discipleship. Baptism, we will find, is not the culmination of faith but its inception—an inaugural step in a lifelong journey of discipleship. We will witness how it marks not only the beginning of the path but a continuous commitment to follow Christ's teachings, to walk in newness of life.

As we embark on this chapter, let the echoes of the Great Commission reverberate within you—a command that invites us to make disciples, to baptize, and to teach. Baptism, as we will discover, is not just a solitary act; it is a catalyst for a life dedicated to discipleship, a profound response to Christ's command that continues to shape the transformative act of water baptism in the Christian faith.

The Biblical Foundation of the Great Commission

In the annals of Christian history, few directives carry the weight and significance of the Great Commission. As we embark on the first topic of this chapter, we find ourselves standing on hallowed ground—the biblical foundation of this monumental command.

Our journey commences in the Gospel of Matthew, where we encounter the words of Jesus echoing through the ages: "Go therefore and make disciples of all nations, baptizing them in the name of the Father and of the Son and of the Holy Spirit, teaching them to observe all that I have commanded you" (Matthew 28:19–20). These words, spoken by our Lord and Savior, provide the cornerstone of the Great Commission, and they resonate with an authority that reverberates through the centuries.

To understand the full significance of this command, we must delve into its historical and cultural context. In the time of Christ, baptism was not a foreign concept; rather, it was a well-established ritual. The Jews practiced ritual purification through immersion in mikveh baths, and John the Baptist had ushered in a baptism of repentance. Against this backdrop, Jesus's directive to baptize in the name of the Father, Son, and Holy Spirit signaled a transformation—an expansion of the ancient ritual into a symbol of faith in the triune God.

As we immerse ourselves in the historical and cultural tapestry of this command, we begin to grasp its profound significance within the Christian faith. Baptism becomes not merely an act of obedience but a means of initiation into the family of God, a declaration of one's allegiance to the Father, the Son, and the Holy Spirit. It is a tangible expression of faith in the triune nature of God—a faith that binds believers across time and space.

In this exploration of the biblical foundation of the Great Commission, we stand on the precipice of a sacred journey— one that compels us to go forth, to make disciples, and to baptize in the name of the triune God. It is an invitation to embrace the weighty responsibility and the immense privilege of carrying out Christ's command, a command that bridges the ancient past with the contemporary present, and that continues to shape the transformative act of water baptism in the Christian faith.

════════

The Story of Pastor Abraham
and the Village Revival

Pastor Abraham, a seasoned missionary in the rural expanses of East Africa, knew the power of the Great Commission firsthand. At 58, he had spent decades preaching and teaching, but one particular mission deepened his understanding of the biblical directive to baptize and make disciples.

In a small village where water was scarce and spiritual hunger even more profound, Pastor Samuel arrived with a team ready to dig wells and share the gospel. The villagers, primarily followers of traditional beliefs, were initially skeptical of the newcomers. However, they were desperate for clean water and intrigued by the missionaries' promise of "living water."

As the physical well neared completion, Pastor Abraham began teaching the villagers about Jesus, using the freshly translated local language Bibles. He focused on Matthew 28:19–20, explaining how Jesus commanded His followers to make disciples and baptize them in the name of the Father, Son, and Holy Spirit. The villagers listened, captivated by the stories of Jesus and moved by the parallels drawn between the life-giving water from their new well and the spiritual renewal baptism represented.

One evening, as the sun set over the newly completed well, Pastor Abraham held the first baptism service. A dozen villagers, including Kofi, the village elder, stepped forward. As they were baptized, Kofi spoke of feeling a new birth, a cleansing not just of body but of spirit. This act of baptism, conducted in the dusty basin of their new well, symbolized their acceptance into a larger family beyond their village—a global community of believers.

The impact of that day resonated throughout the village and beyond. The baptism became a testament to their faith, leading to a revival in the village. Families that had once been divided by belief began to unite under the teachings of Christ. The village transformed, using their resources not only to sustain themselves but also to help neighboring communities.

Years later, Kofi's son, now a young man, would take up Pastor Abraham's mantle, traveling to other villages with the same message and mission. He carried with him the legacy of that transformative moment by the well, driven by the Great Commission's call to make disciples and baptize, just as Pastor Abraham had done for his father and many others.

This story, rooted in the obedience to Christ's command, highlights the profound value of the Great Commission. It is not merely a call to convert but a mandate to transform communities by integrating the spiritual with the everyday, the ancient with the contemporary, and by doing so, perpetuating the cycle of faith and renewal that transcends generations.

Baptism as a Public Declaration of Faith

In the profound tapestry of Christian faith, baptism emerges as not just a private ritual but a powerful public declaration— a topic we explore in the second segment of this chapter. As we wade into the waters of this topic, we are reminded that the act of baptism is far more than a solitary experience; it is a profound testimony of one's commitment to follow Jesus.

Imagine standing at the water's edge, surrounded by a congregation of witnesses. This collective assembly bears testimony to a profound truth—that baptism is not a clandestine affair but a public spectacle, a declaration of faith in the presence of fellow believers. In Acts 8:12, we glimpse the early believers' practice of baptism: "But when they believed Philip as he preached good news about the kingdom of God and the name of Jesus Christ, they were baptized, both men and women."

This passage illustrates the inseparable connection between faith and baptism—the recognition that belief in Christ naturally leads to the public declaration of that faith through baptism. It is a testimony that transcends the individual, inviting others to bear witness to a soul's commitment to follow Jesus. Baptism becomes a proclamation of allegiance, a banner unfurled before the community of faith.

To illustrate the power of baptism as a public declaration, we turn to the story of Mark, a young man who, after years of searching, found faith in Christ. His decision to be baptized was not a quiet, solitary event.

Instead, it was a moment shared with his church family— a moment that echoed with the words of Romans 6:4: "We were buried therefore with him by baptism into death, in order that, just as Christ was raised from the dead by the glory of the Father, we too might walk in newness of life."

Mark's baptism was not merely a personal experience; it was a public witness to his commitment to walk in newness of life, to be identified with Christ's death and resurrection. His baptism invited others to join in the celebration of his faith, reinforcing the truth that baptism is a communal expression of devotion.

As we navigate the waters of baptism as a public declaration of faith, we encounter countless stories of individuals who have used this sacred rite as a powerful testimony. From the first Christians in the book of Acts to contemporary believers worldwide, the act of baptism serves as a beacon—a declaration that faith is not merely a private matter but a communal, public confession. It is an invitation for all to bear witness to the transformative power of Christ's grace and the commitment to follow Him.

In the chapters that follow, we will continue to explore the multifaceted significance of baptism within the context of the Great Commission. Baptism, we will find, is not only a personal act of faith but a communal celebration—a public declaration of allegiance to the Lord, a proclamation that echoes through time and space.

―――――――

The Story of Savannah and the
Community Baptism

In the small coastal town of Clearwater, where the community church bell can be heard across the quiet streets every Sunday, Savannah, a 33-year-old teacher, found herself at a crossroads in life. Having moved to the town seeking a fresh start after a tumultuous period, she initially kept to herself, hesitant to engage with her new neighbors or their traditions.

One summer day, as the town prepared for its annual community baptism event at the local river, Savannah's curiosity got the better of her. The event was described in flyers as a celebration of faith, a public affirmation of personal and communal commitment to follow the teachings of Jesus Christ. It piqued her interest, and for the first time, she felt a pull towards understanding more about this collective expression of faith.

As she approached the riverbank, Savannah was struck by the sight. People from all walks of life, families, elderly residents, and young adults like herself, gathered with a sense of purpose and joy. She saw individuals stepping forward, publicly declaring their faith, and being baptized in the open waters, surrounded by supportive cheers and prayers from the community. It was a powerful scene of unity and openness, quite unlike the private, introspective way she had viewed faith up to that point.

Moved by the ceremony and the palpable sense of community support, Savannah sought out the pastor, a gentle man known for his welcoming spirit and wise words. He spoke to her about the significance of baptism not just as a personal milestone, but as a vibrant declaration of one's faith before family, friends, and neighbors. He quoted Acts 8:12, emphasizing how baptism in the early Church was a public testament to one's belief and commitment to follow Christ.

Encouraged by their conversation, Savannah decided to take a step of faith. The following year, at the same event, she stood at the river's edge, ready to make her own public declaration. Her decision to be baptized was not made in isolation; it was a commitment made in the presence of an entire community that had shown her an incredible outpouring of support and acceptance.

As Savannah emerged from the water, the cheers from the crowd filled her with a renewed sense of belonging and purpose. Her baptism became more than just a spiritual rebirth; it was a moment of profound connection with her community. It reinforced the idea that her faith journey was not just a personal endeavor but a journey supported by and intertwined with the lives of those around her.

In the months and years that followed, Savannah became an active member of the community. She realized that her baptism was not the end but the beginning of a deeper engagement with her faith and her neighbors. It was a public testament that continually reminded her of the community's strength and the shared path they walked in faith.

Through Savannah's story, the profound impact of baptism as a public declaration of faith is vividly illustrated. It shows how this act of faith, witnessed by a community, not only transforms an individual but strengthens the bonds within the community, creating a shared narrative of faith, renewal, and commitment. This narrative reinforces the truth that baptism is not merely a solitary or private event but a communal celebration and a powerful public statement of belonging and belief in the journey of faith.

―――――

The Role of Baptism in Discipleship

As we continue our exploration of baptism within the framework of the Great Commission, we now embark on a journey that uncovers the profound role of baptism in the discipleship process. Baptism, we discover, is not a solitary event but the inaugural step in a lifelong journey of faith—a journey marked by an unwavering commitment to follow Christ's teachings.

Picture a disciple standing at the water's edge, about to take the plunge into the baptismal waters. It is a momentous occasion, not just because it symbolizes a believer's faith in Christ but because it signifies the beginning of a profound discipleship journey. In Matthew 28:19–20, Jesus commands His followers to make disciples, "baptizing them in the name of the Father and of the Son and of the Holy Spirit, teaching them to observe all that I have commanded you."

This directive paints a vivid picture of discipleship intertwined with baptism. Baptism is not a mere rite of passage; it is the entry point into a lifelong commitment to follow Christ's teachings. Just as Christ's disciples were called to baptize and teach, modern believers are summoned to embrace baptism as the commencement of a faith journey—a journey where Christ's teachings become the guiding principles of life.

To illustrate the role of baptism in discipleship, we turn to the story of Rachel, a young woman who, after being baptized, embarked on a journey of spiritual growth and transformation. Her baptism was not the culmination of her faith but the starting point—a decisive step that marked her commitment to follow Christ's teachings. Again, just as Romans 6:4 reminds us, "We were buried therefore with him by baptism into death, in order that, just as Christ was raised from the dead by the glory of the Father, we too might walk in newness of life."

Rachel's baptism was a declaration of her desire to walk in newness of life, to be molded by the teachings of Christ. It symbolized not only her faith but her dedication to the ongoing process of discipleship—a process that involves learning, growing, and continually aligning one's life with the teachings of Jesus.

As we delve deeper into the role of baptism in discipleship, we recognize that it is not a one-time event but an ongoing expression of faith and commitment. It is the commencement of a lifelong journey where believers immerse themselves in the teachings of Christ, seeking to live out His commands day by day.

In the chapters that follow, we will continue to explore the multifaceted significance of baptism within the context of the Great Commission. Baptism is not merely a solitary act but the inaugural step in a discipleship journey—a declaration that faith is not static but dynamic, an invitation to follow Christ's teachings with unwavering devotion and obedience.

The Transformation of Elisha: From Isolation to Discipleship

Elisha, a 40-year-old software developer, had always approached life with a skeptic's eye, especially towards matters of faith. Raised in a secular home, the concept of spiritual belief was foreign to him, more a subject of intellectual debate than personal relevance. However, a series of life-changing events, including a severe illness that brought him to the brink of despair, prompted Elisha to seek deeper meanings beyond the tangible world.

His journey towards faith began unassumingly, through friendships formed at a local coffee shop with individuals who not only debated religion but lived their faith actively. Their discussions often revolved around the teachings of Christ and the Christian practice of baptism as a symbol of new life. Intrigued and seeking a fresh start after his recovery, Elisha attended a church service where the sermon on discipleship struck a profound chord within him.

Moved by the message and the communal spirit of the congregation, Elisha decided to take the plunge—both metaphorically and literally. His decision to be baptized was not an end but a vibrant beginning. On the day of his baptism, standing before the waters, he felt a mix of anticipation and serenity. As he was submerged, the cold rush of water seemed to wash away years of doubt and isolation.

Emerging from the water, Elisha experienced what many describe as a rebirth. He was not only declaring his new-found faith publicly but also stepping into a journey of discipleship. This act of baptism marked his commitment to learning and living according to Christ's teachings. It was, as Matthew 28:19–20 outlines, his initiation into a life of actively following and growing in the teachings of Jesus.

Post-baptism, Elisha's journey did not smooth out magically, but the challenges he faced were now undergirded by a community and a framework of faith. He joined a discipleship group in his church, where he learned the essence of living out the teachings of Christ daily. The group met weekly, diving deep into biblical studies and supporting one another through life's highs and lows.

Elisha's story became one of transformation and influence. His baptism, initially a personal milestone, evolved into a communal journey as he began to mentor new believers in the church. His home, once a place of solitude, now regularly hosted gatherings where discussions of faith and life intermingled.

In Elisha, the role of baptism transcended the act itself; it was the gateway to a life marked by growth, community, and active discipleship. His story highlights how baptism, as the inaugural step in discipleship, is not merely a ritual but a continuous, living commitment to follow and apply the teachings of Christ in every aspect of life.

Through his narrative, we see the multifaceted significance of baptism within the framework of the Great Commission: it is a profound declaration of faith, a commitment to lifelong learning, and a dynamic journey of spiritual growth. It reminds us that baptism is the beginning of a transformational path where each step, each day, is an opportunity to embody the teachings of Jesus, leading by example and fostering a community of faith and discipleship.

Conclusion

As we conclude our journey through the waters of Chapter 3, "The Great Commission: Baptism as Christ's Command," we find ourselves at the confluence of faith and action, belief and obedience. This chapter has been a voyage into the heart of the Christian mission, where the words of Jesus, the Great Commission, serve as our compass.

We began by standing on the banks of scripture, where Matthew 28:16–20 beckoned us to make disciples, to baptize, and to teach—all under the authority of the triune God. In this sacred command, we unearthed the foundation upon which the transformative act of baptism stands.

Baptism, we learned, is not a solitary event but a communal expression of faith, a public declaration of one's commitment to follow Christ. Through stories like that of Rachel, we witnessed how baptism marks the inception of a lifelong journey of discipleship. It is the first step in a path where believers immerse themselves in the teachings of Christ, walking in newness of life. Baptism, as we've discovered, is not a one-time ritual but an ongoing expression of faith, a commitment to live out the commands of Jesus.

As we bid farewell to this chapter, we carry with us the profound truth that baptism is not a mere tradition but a transformative response to Christ's command. It is an invitation to make disciples, to embrace the Great Commission as our own, and to walk alongside others in their faith journey. Baptism calls us to a discipleship that transcends the waters, shaping our lives as we follow the teachings of Christ, day by day.

In the chapters ahead, we will continue to delve deeper into the transformative act of water baptism, exploring its contemporary relevance, its symbolism, and the stories of those who have been forever changed by these sacred waters. But for now, let the resonance of this chapter linger—a call to discipleship, a testament to the enduring significance of baptism, and an invitation to follow in the footsteps of our Savior.

CHAPTER FOUR

The Baptismal Vow: A Public Declaration of a Private Faith

"For all of you who were baptized into Christ have clothed yourselves
with Christ." —GALATIANS 3:27 NIV

I n the quiet sanctity of baptismal waters, a profound
dialogue unfolds—a dialogue of promises, commitments,
and unwavering faith. In this chapter, we embark on a journey
into the heart of the Christian experience—the baptismal vow.
It is here, at the intersection of personal faith and communal
affirmation, that we encounter the transformative power of
sacred promises. As we wade into the depths of this chapter,
we explore the significance of the baptismal vow, unearthing

its biblical and historical origins, and discovering how it bridges the realm of private belief with the public declaration of allegiance to Christ.

The baptismal vow, like a radiant jewel, gleams with spiritual significance. It is more than a recitation of words; it is a solemn commitment—an agreement with God, a covenant that unites not only the individual with the divine but also the faith community in a shared journey of faith.

Through the lens of scripture, we will unravel the depths of these vows and witness how they signify a profound turning point in one's faith journey. Moreover, we will explore the beauty of the baptismal covenant, where promises made echo with echoes of divine grace and communal support, forming a sacred bond that sustains and nurtures the believer's walk with Christ.

Finally, we will journey through the diverse landscape of Christian traditions, witnessing how various denominations approach baptismal vows, recognizing both the distinctions and the commonalities that affirm the transformative power of these sacred promises. As we embark on this exploration, may the echoes of the baptismal vow resound within us, a testament to the fusion of individual faith with the rich tapestry of the Christian community, and an affirmation that these sacred words hold the potential to change lives and hearts.

The Significance of the Baptismal Vow

In the depths of baptism's sacred waters lies a profound and solemn moment—the making of vows and promises. These words are not mere formalities but sacred affirmations of faith, connecting the private realm of belief to the public declaration of allegiance to Christ. As we dive into the first topic of this chapter, we unravel the significance of the baptismal vow, tracing its roots through biblical and historical passages that illuminate its role in affirming one's faith in Christ.

Our journey begins with the understanding that baptism is not a passive act but a dynamic response to the gospel. In Acts 2:38, we see Peter's call to action, "Repent and be baptized, every one of you, in the name of Jesus Christ for the forgiveness of your sins." Here, baptism is intrinsically linked to repentance—a turning away from sin and a turning toward Christ. This call to repentance underscores the gravity of the promises made during baptism; they are not empty words but a genuine commitment to follow Jesus.

To comprehend the origins of the baptismal vow, we delve into the rich tapestry of scripture, where we find baptism intertwined with faith. Romans 10:9 proclaims, "If you confess with your mouth that Jesus is Lord and believe in your heart that God raised him from the dead, you will be saved." This confession of faith forms the core of the baptismal vow—a heartfelt acknowledgment that Jesus is Lord and Savior, a belief etched into the very fabric of one's being.

But the significance of these vows extends beyond the pages of the New Testament; it reverberates through the corridors of history. Early Christian writings, such as the Didache, shed light on the baptismal vows practiced by the earliest believers. These vows were not a matter of tradition but a tangible expression of faith, a declaration before witnesses that faith in Christ had taken root.

As we journey deeper into the importance of the baptismal vow, we recognize that these promises serve as a bridge between the private and public aspects of faith. They signify a commitment to Christ—a commitment that echoes through the ages, unifying believers in a shared confession of faith.

In the chapters that follow, we will continue to explore the multifaceted role of these vows within the baptismal covenant, emphasizing their power to affirm and strengthen one's faith in Christ, transforming a private belief into a public declaration.

―――――

Echoes of Faith: The Transformative Journey of Baptismal Vows

In a quaint village nestled between rolling hills and flowing rivers, there lived a young woman named Avery. Avery had been raised in a devout Christian family, and faith had always been a quiet, personal aspect of her life. Her relationship with

God was heartfelt, but like the still waters of the secluded lake near her home, her faith was private and undisturbed.

As Avery grew into adulthood, she found herself grappling with deeper questions about her faith and the role it should play in her life. Her journey of introspection led her to her community's old stone church, where she had attended services since childhood but had never fully engaged beyond the weekly rituals.

One Sunday, after a particularly stirring sermon on the significance of baptismal vows, Avery felt a tug in her soul. The pastor spoke passionately about Acts 2:38 and the transformative promise of baptism—not just as a ritual, but as a public declaration of faith and a personal commitment to follow Christ's teachings.

Moved by this message, Avery decided to take a step that she had postponed since her youth—she chose to be baptized. The decision was more than just participating in a ceremony; it was about publicly affirming her faith and vocally embracing the vows of baptism as her own commitment to Christ.

On the day of her baptism, the village gathered at the church, the air filled with a sense of communal warmth. As Avery stepped into the baptismal font, she felt the weight of the moment—the cold water not just signifying purification, but enveloping her in a new beginning. She repeated the baptismal vows, her voice steady and more confident with each word, declaring her faith openly for the first time.

"I confess with my mouth that Jesus is Lord and believe in my heart that God raised him from the dead," she proclaimed, echoing Romans 10:9. This public confession was not merely a formality but a powerful affirmation of her belief, witnessed by her community.

The impact of Avery's baptism extended beyond the walls of the church. Her public declaration inspired others in the village, especially the youth, who saw in her a genuine example of living faith. Avery became more involved in church activities, leading youth groups and helping to organize community outreach programs. Her baptism had transformed her private faith into a dynamic and public testament to her commitment to Christ.

Avery's story highlights the profound impact of the baptismal vow—not just as words recited during a ritual but as a lifelong commitment that strengthens personal faith and influences the wider community. Her journey from private belief to public declaration exemplifies the transformative power of openly embracing and living out the promises made at baptism.

———

The Baptismal Covenant: Understanding the Commitment

Amidst the sacred waters of baptism, something profound transpires—a covenant takes shape. In the second topic of this chapter, we plunge into the heart of the baptismal covenant, an agreement that binds not only the individual but also the faith community and God Himself. Here, we explore the intricacies of this sacred pact, examining the vows and commitments made by both the baptized person and the faith community to support and nurture the faith journey.

The baptismal covenant is a tapestry woven with threads of faith, commitment, and community—a covenant that mirrors the divine covenant between God and His people. As we navigate its depths, we find ourselves in the company of believers who, like Abraham of old, respond to God's call with faith and obedience. Just as God entered into a covenant with Abraham, promising to be his God and the God of his descendants, the baptismal covenant signifies God's commitment to the baptized person and their spiritual journey.

This divine covenant is mirrored in the vows and commitments made during baptism, encapsulating the essence of Romans 12:5: "So we, though many, are one body in Christ, and individually members one of another." In this union, the individual pledges to follow Christ, to walk in His ways, and to be a faithful disciple. Simultaneously, the faith community pledges support and nurture—a promise that echoes the apostle Paul's exhortation in Galatians 6:2: "Bear one another's burdens, and so fulfill the law of Christ."

Through the baptismal covenant, we see a beautiful synergy between the individual's faith journey and the collective responsibility of the faith community. Just as baptism signifies a personal commitment, it also signifies an acknowledgment of the interconnectedness of believers. In the act of baptism, the person professes their faith, the faith community pledges support, and God extends His grace and guidance.

To illuminate the significance of this covenant, we turn to the story of Sarah, a young woman who, upon her baptism, not only committed to following Christ but also found herself embraced by a community of believers who vowed to walk alongside her in her faith journey. Her baptism was a reminder that she was not alone, that her faith was not isolated but part of a larger tapestry of believers—a family in Christ.

As we conclude our exploration of the baptismal covenant, we recognize that it is not a solitary act but a communal agreement—a sacred bond that unites the individual, the faith community, and God in a commitment to nurture and sustain the faith journey. In the chapters ahead, we will continue to unveil the transformative power of this covenant within the context of baptism, emphasizing its role in strengthening faith and fostering a sense of belonging within the family of God.

The Bond of Water and Promise:
The Story of Levi

In the bustling community of Brooklyn, New York, Levi, a 28-year-old graphic designer, felt the pull of a deeper calling amidst the noise of his everyday routines. Despite his successful career and active social life, there was a yearning for something more meaningful, a connection that seemed just out of reach.

Levi's journey toward spiritual fulfillment began unexpectedly at a friend's baptism service. Witnessing the ceremony, he was struck by the powerful sense of community and the profound commitments being voiced. It wasn't just the act of baptism that moved him; it was the baptismal covenant—the shared promises between the individual being baptized, the community, and God.

Motivated by what he saw, Levi decided to take the step himself. As he prepared for his baptism, he delved into the meaning behind the vows, learning about the covenant that would not only bind him to his faith more deeply but also connect him with a community ready to support him.

On the day of his baptism, standing before the gathered congregation, Levi felt a surge of emotions. As he professed his faith and was submerged in the waters, there was a palpable sense of dying to his old self and emerging renewed. But more impactful was the response from the community. They didn't just witness his baptism; they actively pledged to support him, echoing the words of Galatians 6:2, "Bear one another's burdens, and so fulfill the law of Christ."

This collective commitment resonated deeply with Levi. It was not just about his personal declaration of faith but about becoming part of a body that promised to walk with him, guide him, and support him. This mutual pledge was the essence of the baptismal covenant—a promise of shared journeys and mutual aid, reflecting the interconnectedness of their faith.

The transformation in Levi was profound. He became more involved in his church, engaging in various ministries and outreach programs. His faith journey was no longer a solo endeavor but was supported by the strength of community bonds, reinforcing his commitment to live out the teachings of Christ daily.

Levi's story is a testament to the transformative power of the baptismal covenant. It illustrates how baptism transcends individual spiritual experiences, fostering a strong community network that upholds each member. This synergy between personal faith and communal support not only nurtures the individual's spiritual growth but also strengthens the fabric of the entire faith community, making each baptism not just a moment of personal commitment but a celebration of collective faith and support.

Baptismal Vows in Different Christian Traditions

As we journey through the diverse tapestry of Christian traditions, we encounter a beautiful mosaic of beliefs and practices surrounding baptismal vows—the subject of our third exploration in this chapter. Each denomination, with its unique history and theological perspectives, approaches baptismal vows in its distinct way, often diverging in wording, rituals, and theological nuances. Yet, beneath these surface differences lies a common thread—a shared affirmation of the transformative power inherent in the act of making these sacred promises.

In the realm of Christian traditions, baptismal vows are like keys, unlocking the doors to deeper spiritual understanding and commitment. The Orthodox tradition, for instance, celebrates the "renunciation of Satan" as part of the vows—a powerful declaration of turning away from darkness and embracing the light of Christ. In the words of James 4:7, we find resonance: "Submit yourselves therefore to God. Resist the devil, and he will flee from you." This renunciation is a profound step in breaking the chains of the enemy and embracing the liberating grace of Christ.

In contrast, the Protestant tradition often emphasizes personal faith and profession of belief, echoing the teachings of Romans 10:9: "If you confess with your mouth that Jesus is Lord and believe in your heart that God raised him from the dead, you will be saved." This confession of faith stands at the heart of many Protestant baptismal vows—a public declaration that Jesus is Lord and Savior.

Catholic tradition, on the other hand, highlights the role of godparents in making promises on behalf of the baptized child—a beautiful reminder of the communal nature of faith. Just as 1 Corinthians 12:26 states, "If one member suffers, all suffer together; if one member is honored, all rejoice together."

The Catholic baptismal vows symbolize the interconnectedness of the body of Christ.

Despite these distinctions, a unifying thread runs through all Christian traditions—the recognition that baptismal vows are not mere words but profound commitments to walk in the footsteps of Christ. They signify a pledge to follow His teachings, to be part of His body, and to be transformed by His grace. Whether immersed in the waters of a Baptist church, anointed in a Catholic cathedral, or immersed three times in the name of the Father, Son, and Holy Spirit in an Orthodox font, the transformative power of these vows remains a constant, bridging the diverse expressions of faith.

In this exploration of baptismal vows across Christian traditions, we discover that, beyond the rituals and denominational differences, a deep resonance exists. The transformative power of these vows transcends theological nuances, uniting believers in a shared commitment to follow Christ. In the chapters ahead, we will continue to uncover the layers of significance embedded in the baptismal vow—a vow that bridges the individual's faith with the community of believers and connects them all to the transformative grace of Christ.

Unity in Diversity: The Story of Camila

In the heart of Toronto's multicultural landscape, Camila, a 34-year-old ecumenical theologian, embarked on a mission to bridge denominational divides. Her journey was inspired by her profound appreciation for the diverse practices of baptismal vows across Christian traditions, recognizing them as a testament to the universal call of faith despite their differences.

Camila organized a series of ecumenical forums titled "Waters That Bind: Exploring Baptismal Vows Across Traditions." These forums were designed to bring together leaders and laypeople from Orthodox, Protestant, and Catholic communities to share and learn about each other's baptismal practices. Her goal was not just to inform but to foster a sense of unity among the disparate Christian communities within the city.

The first forum featured an Orthodox priest who discussed the profound symbolism of the "renunciation of Satan" in Orthodox baptismal vows, emphasizing the spiritual warfare aspect of the Christian journey. This resonated with many attendees, particularly highlighting the verse from James 4:7, "Submit yourselves therefore to God. Resist the devil, and he will flee from you."

Next, a Protestant pastor shared how their tradition focuses on a personal declaration of faith, echoing Romans 10:9, "If you confess with your mouth that Jesus is Lord and believe in your heart that God raised him from the dead, you will be saved." This emphasis on personal conviction and declaration sparked discussions on the role of personal testimony in spiritual life.

The series culminated with a presentation by a Catholic priest who explained the role of godparents in making baptismal promises on behalf of infants. He tied this to the communal nature of faith as reflected in 1 Corinthians 12:26, "If one member suffers, all suffer together; if one member is honored, all rejoice together." This highlighted the interconnectedness and supportive dynamics of the faith community.

Throughout these sessions, Camila facilitated discussions that allowed participants to delve deeper into the significance of these vows, not just as theological statements but as commitments that bind the community together, regardless of denominational lines. The forums became a space for sharing, understanding, and appreciating the rich tapestry of Christian faith practices.

The impact of Camila's initiative was profound. Participants left with a renewed sense of unity and commitment to the shared core of their faith. They recognized that despite the different expressions of baptismal vows, the underlying commitment to follow Christ and support one another in the faith journey was a powerful common ground.

Camila's story highlights the transformative power of understanding and respecting religious diversity within the

Christian community. It showcases how baptism, a sacred act embedded in tradition and commitment, can serve as a bridge, uniting diverse believers under the banner of shared faith and mutual support. This unity, fostered through the exploration of baptismal vows, strengthens the individual's faith journey and enriches the broader Christian community.

Conclusion

As we conclude our deep dive into the sacred realm of baptismal vows in Chapter 4, we emerge from the waters with a profound understanding of their significance. These vows, uttered in the presence of God and the faith community, stand as a testament to the transformative power of faith in action.

We began our journey by uncovering the biblical and historical origins of these vows, recognizing that they are not mere words but tangible commitments—a solemn bridge between the individual's private faith and the public declaration of allegiance to Christ. Our exploration revealed that, regardless of the specific wording or rituals, the essence of these vows remains steadfast—an unwavering pledge to follow Jesus.

We then ventured into the heart of the baptismal covenant, where these promises take on a deeper significance. This covenant, encompassing the individual, the faith community, and God Himself, mirrors the divine covenant between God and His people. It signifies not only a personal commitment but also a recognition of the interconnectedness of believers— a commitment to support and nurture one another's faith journey.

Our exploration culminated in a panoramic view of baptismal vows across different Christian traditions. While nuances and rituals may differ, a common thread of commitment and transformation runs through them all. These vows, whether recited in the solemnity of an Orthodox font, the simplicity of a Protestant church, or the community embrace of a Catholic cathedral, hold the power to shape lives and deepen faith.

As we step away from the baptismal waters of this chapter, we carry with us the resonance of these sacred promises—a testament to the enduring significance of faith in action. In the chapters ahead, we will continue to delve deeper into the transformative act of water baptism, exploring its contemporary relevance, its symbolism, and the stories of those who have been forever changed by these sacred waters.

But for now, let the echoes of the baptismal vow linger— a call to commitment, a declaration of faith, and a testament to the transformative grace of Christ.

CHAPTER FIVE

Submerged in Commitment: The Act and Art of Full Immersion

"Having been buried with him in baptism, in which you were also raised with him through your faith in the working of God, who raised him from the dead." —COLOSSIANS 2:12 NIV

In the stillness of a sanctuary, beneath the watchful eyes of a congregation, or amidst the natural beauty of a riverbank, a profound ritual unfolds—a ritual that has traversed centuries and continents, uniting believers across the ages. It is the act of full immersion baptism, a sacred journey that transcends the mundane and delves deep into the spiritual realm. In this chapter, we embark on an exploration of full immersion, a practice that embodies the essence of faith, commitment, and transformation.

Full immersion baptism is more than a mere ritual; it is a spiritual voyage—a metaphorical odyssey undertaken by believers as they descend into the waters and rise anew. It symbolizes the death of the old self and the resurrection into a new life in Christ, an act that finds its roots in the very pages of Scripture.

Our journey begins with the theological depth of full immersion. We delve into the profound significance of this mode of baptism, where a believer is completely submerged in water. Through the lens of scripture, we will uncover how full immersion mirrors the imagery of death and resurrection—a concept deeply embedded in the Christian faith. We will draw parallels with biblical passages and early Christian practices, illuminating the spiritual richness inherent in this act.

But full immersion is not only theological; it is also practical. It requires meticulous preparation and careful execution. From the filling of the baptismal pool to the ceremonial aspects, each detail is essential in ensuring a smooth and meaningful immersion experience. The act of full immersion baptism is a choreographed dance between faith and practice, where physical preparations mirror the readiness of the believer's heart to be immersed in Christ's redemptive grace.

Ceremony and symbolism play a significant role in full immersion baptism. We will explore the rituals and symbols embedded in this sacred act, each adding depth and meaning to the experience. Just as Christ was buried and raised, so too is the believer symbolically buried beneath the waters and brought forth as a new creation. We will draw connections to biblical narratives and share personal testimonials that resonate with the transformative power of this symbolic journey.

As we journey through this chapter, the waters of full immersion will reveal their depths—a depth of theology, of preparation, of symbolism, and of personal transformation. We invite you to immerse yourself in the art and act of full immersion baptism, to explore the timeless and enduring significance of this sacred rite that continues to shape the faith and commitment of believers around the world.

Theology of Full Immersion

In the baptismal font's embrace, we encounter more than mere water; we are immersed in a profound theological journey. In our exploration of the first topic of this chapter, we plunge into the theological depths of full immersion baptism. This mode of baptism, where a believer is completely submerged in water, symbolizes far more than a ritual—it signifies a profound cleansing and transformation of the soul. To fathom its significance, we draw from biblical passages and the practices of early Christians, revealing the spiritual richness inherent in this act.

Full immersion baptism, as we unveil its theological layers, mirrors the imagery of death and resurrection—a concept deeply embedded in the Christian faith. In Romans 6:4, we are reminded, "We were buried therefore with him by baptism into death, in order that, just as Christ was raised from the dead by the glory of the Father, we too might walk in newness of life." This passage illuminates the transformative power of full immersion as we descend into the waters, symbolizing the burial of the old self and emerge, rising anew in Christ's resurrection—a powerful declaration of rebirth.

Moreover, we find parallels in the Old Testament, particularly in the story of the Israelites' passage through the Red Sea. As 1 Corinthians 10:2 notes, "They were all baptized into Moses in the cloud and in the sea." The crossing of the Red Sea was not merely a physical journey but a spiritual one—a transition from bondage to freedom, from the old life to a new one. In the same vein, full immersion baptism signifies a crossing over from a life dominated by sin to a life embraced by the grace of Christ.

To further understand the theological significance of full immersion, we delve into the practices of early Christians, who closely followed the apostles' teachings. The Didache, one of the earliest Christian writings, provides instructions for baptism, emphasizing full immersion as the norm. This practice echoed the apostolic tradition, underscoring the theological depth of this mode of baptism within the early church.

In our exploration of the theology of full immersion, we uncover a profound symbolism—an act of total surrender and rebirth. Full immersion baptism is more than a ritual; it is a testament to the transformative power of faith in Christ. As we continue our journey through this chapter, we will dive deeper into the practical aspects of full immersion, unveiling the intricate preparations, ceremonies, and the symbolic journey that culminates in the emergence of a new creation in Christ.

Submerging into New Beginnings: Gianna's Renewal Through Full Immersion

Gianna, a 34-year-old graphic designer, felt adrift in a sea of uncertainty and past regrets. Although successful in her career, her personal life was marred by choices that left her feeling disconnected from her earlier, more hopeful self. The desire for a fresh start led her to a community church, intrigued by their practice of full immersion baptism—a symbol of profound spiritual renewal.

At the church, Gianna learned that baptism was not merely a formality but a transformative journey mirrored in the depths of water. The pastor explained how this sacred act of full immersion represented the burial of the old self and a resurrection to new life, as depicted in Romans 6:4. Inspired, Gianna decided to take the plunge, seeking both forgiveness and a new direction in her life.

On the day of her baptism, surrounded by supportive faces and the tranquil sounds of a flowing river, Gianna stepped into the water. The cool embrace of the river was not just physical but profoundly spiritual. As she was submerged, her heart released the burdens of her past; rising from the water, she felt an overwhelming sense of rebirth—her slate wiped clean, her spirit invigorated.

This pivotal moment was not the end but the beginning of Gianna's journey. The baptism was a public declaration of her new-found commitment to live differently. The church community, having witnessed her vow, rallied around her, offering support and fellowship that reinforced her transformation.

Gianna's story spread within the community, inspiring others who felt shackled by their pasts to consider baptism as a pathway to renewal. Her experience highlighted the powerful symbolism of full immersion—not just as a theological concept but as a practical manifestation of faith's capacity to alter lives profoundly.

Through her journey, Gianna discovered that the waters of baptism do more than cleanse; they offer a chance to rise anew, embodying the transformative promise of faith and community in the pursuit of a fulfilled and purposeful life.

The Practical Aspects of Full Immersion

As we journey deeper into the waters of full immersion baptism, we find ourselves amidst the practical nuances of this profound rite. In the second topic of this chapter, we delve into the practical aspects that underpin the act of full immersion. From physical preparations to ceremonial considerations, and the pivotal role of baptizers, we unravel the intricacies that contribute to a smooth and deeply meaningful immersion experience.

The act of full immersion baptism is a carefully choreographed dance between faith and practice, where the waters of theology meet the shores of logistics. The physical preparations for this sacred event are akin to John the Baptist's call in Matthew 3:3, "Prepare the way of the Lord; make his paths straight." Just as John prepared the way for Christ's ministry, believers prepare for baptism by ensuring the baptismal pool is ready—a pool filled with water that will serve as a vessel of transformation. These preparations, though practical, hold immense spiritual significance, as they signify the readiness of the believer's heart to be immersed in Christ's redemptive grace.

Ceremonially, full immersion baptism is a tapestry woven with symbols and rituals, each adding depth to the experience. It mirrors the symbolism of Christ's death, burial, and resurrection, an act that Paul speaks of in 1 Corinthians 15:3–4: "For I delivered to you as of first importance what I also received: that Christ died for our sins in accordance with the Scriptures, that He was buried, that He was raised on the third day in accordance with the Scriptures." This biblical narrative finds its resonance in the full immersion ceremony—the believer descending into the water (death and burial) and rising up (resurrection) as a new creation.

The role of baptizers in this process is akin to that of a spiritual guide, much like Philip's encounter with the Ethiopian eunuch in Acts 8:36–38. Philip, the baptizer, played a pivotal role in facilitating the Ethiopian's baptism by explaining the scriptures to him. Similarly, those who administer full immersion baptism serve as guides, ensuring that the candidate understands the significance of the act and is fully prepared to make this public declaration of faith.

By investigating the practical aspects of full immersion, we unveil the meticulous care and attention that goes into this sacred rite. Each element, from preparation to ceremony to guidance, plays a crucial role in ensuring a smooth and deeply meaningful immersion experience. As we continue our journey through this chapter, we will explore the symbolic journey of immersion—a journey that transcends the physical act, leading to a profound transformation of the believer's heart and soul.

Harmony of the Sacred Waters: Aaron's
Journey Through Full Immersion

Aaron, a 28-year-old teacher, wrestled with doubts about his life's direction and the depth of his convictions. Amid his search for clarity, he was drawn to the tangible tradition of full immersion baptism, intrigued by its symbolic representation of a complete personal transformation. Encouraged by friends who had undergone similar journeys, Aaron decided to experience baptism himself, seeking not just spiritual renewal but also a public affirmation of his faith.

As Aaron prepared for his baptism, he was involved in every step, from filling the baptismal pool to understanding the symbolic significance behind each ritual. His pastor, serving as his spiritual guide, helped him grasp the profound implications of the act. They discussed the biblical foundations, particularly focusing on 1 Corinthians 15:3–4, emphasizing Christ's death and resurrection as central themes that the baptism ceremony would echo.

On the day of his baptism, the church community gathered around the pool, their presence a comforting reminder of their collective journey and support. Aaron stepped into the water, feeling its cool embrace envelope him, a stark contrast to the warmth of the community's smiles. As he was fully immersed, the quiet under the water was a stark moment of solitude, a brief pause in the world's noise where he could feel a singular connection with his faith.

Emerging from the water, Aaron felt an overwhelming sense of renewal. It was as if the waters had not just washed over his body but through his soul, cleansing him from past regrets and doubts. The ceremony was a public testament to his personal commitment to walk in "newness of life," reflecting the transformative journey described in Romans 6:4.

In the weeks and months that followed, Aaron discovered that his baptism was more than a momentary experience; it was a continual source of strength and reaffirmation. His role in the church grew, as did his involvement in guiding others who were considering baptism. He became a mentor, sharing his story and the practical insights he gained about the preparation and significance of the rite.

Aaron's story became a valued narrative within his community, inspiring others to explore full immersion baptism not just as a tradition, but as a profound commitment to a transformed life. His journey highlighted the seamless integration of theology and practice, where the spiritual grace and community support intersected to create a deeply impactful life event. Through Aaron, many saw that the waters of baptism were not just about the act itself but about the ongoing journey of faith that follows.

===========

The Symbolic Journey of Immersion

As we wade further into the depths of full immersion baptism, we uncover not only its practical intricacies but also its profound symbolic journey. In this third topic of the chapter, we embark on a spiritual odyssey—the metaphorical journey of the believer as they descend into the waters and rise anew.

Full immersion baptism, like a living parable, signifies the death of the old self and the resurrection into new life in Christ. To understand its depth, we draw connections to biblical narratives and personal testimonials that resonate with the transformative power of this sacred act.

The journey of full immersion baptism finds its roots in the powerful imagery of the Bible. In Romans 6:4, the apostle Paul paints a vivid picture: "We were buried therefore with Him by baptism into death, in order that, just as Christ was raised from the dead by the glory of the Father, we too might walk in newness of life." This scripture echoes in the act of immersion—the believer descending beneath the water symbolizing the burial of their old, sinful self, and emerging as a new creation, just as Christ arose from the grave.

This profound symbolism is further illuminated by biblical narratives. Consider the account of the Israelites crossing the Jordan River, as described in Joshua 3:17: "And the priests bearing the ark of the covenant of the Lord stood firmly on dry ground in the midst of the Jordan, and all Israel was passing over on dry ground until all the nation finished passing over the Jordan." Here, the river's waters symbolize the barrier between the wilderness of sin and the promised land of salvation. Similarly, full immersion represents the passage from a life ensnared by sin to a life redeemed and sanctified in Christ.

Personal testimonials also bear witness to the transformative journey of full immersion baptism. Victoria, a believer who recently experienced this rite, shares her story: "As I descended into the water, I felt the weight of my past sins being washed away. When I emerged, it was like being reborn, a fresh start in my faith journey." Victoria's testimony echoes the biblical narrative of death and resurrection and illustrates how full immersion baptism can profoundly impact a believer's spiritual journey.

The symbolic journey of immersion is a profound expression of faith—a physical act that mirrors the spiritual reality of death to sin and resurrection to new life in Christ. Through biblical narratives and personal testimonials, we witness how this act transcends mere ritual, offering believers a tangible experience of transformation. As we continue our exploration, we will dive deeper into the contemporary relevance of full immersion baptism, highlighting its enduring significance in the lives of those who embrace it.

═══════

A New Beginning: Abel's Journey Through
Full Immersion Baptism

Abel's story is one of profound transformation, marked by a pivotal moment of full immersion baptism that redefined his spiritual path and life direction. Once a skeptic, struggling with personal vices and a sense of aimlessness, Abel lived a life that felt increasingly hollow and unfulfilled. Despite his outward success in the corporate world, an inner void persisted, pushing him toward a search for deeper meaning.

The turning point came unexpectedly during a visit to a friend's church. Initially reluctant, Abel was moved by the sermon that discussed the concept of rebirth through baptism, particularly referencing Romans 6:4, which spoke of being "buried with Christ through baptism into death" and rising to "walk in newness of life." This message struck a chord, igniting a spark of hope that perhaps change was possible, even for him.

The decision to undergo full immersion baptism was not made lightly. Abel spent weeks attending baptism classes, engaging with scripture, and reflecting on his life. His preparations were not just logistical but deeply introspective, mirroring the spiritual readiness required for such a significant spiritual commitment.

On the day of his baptism, surrounded by a supportive community, Abel stood at the edge of the baptismal pool, his heart pounding with a mixture of nervousness and excitement.

As he was submerged in the water, he experienced a profound sense of letting go—his old fears, doubts, and failures seemed to dissolve into the depths. Rising from the water, he felt an overwhelming sense of peace and renewal, a symbolic resurrection into a new life centered on Christ's teachings and a commitment to live differently.

Post-baptism, Abel's life reflected his new faith. His relationships improved, he volunteered regularly at community outreach programs, and he found a new purpose in mentoring young adults. His journey of full immersion became a testament within his community, inspiring others with his genuine transformation and his daily commitment to live out his renewed faith.

Abel's story serves as a vivid illustration of the symbolic journey of full immersion baptism—not just as a ritual of faith but as a transformative passage that marks a new beginning, guiding individuals to emerge renewed, just like the Israelites crossed into the promised land, ready to embrace a life aligned with divine purpose.

═══════

Conclusion

As we emerge from the depths of Chapter 5, 'Submerged in Commitment: The Act and Art of Full Immersion," we do so with a richer understanding of the transformative power that lies within the waters of full immersion baptism. In this chapter, we delved into the profound theology, practical considerations, and symbolic journey that define this sacred rite.

Full immersion baptism is a spiritual odyssey—a journey that mirrors the very heart of the Christian faith. It symbolizes the death of the old self and the resurrection into new life in Christ, a truth deeply rooted in the pages of Scripture. From the apostle Paul's vivid imagery in Romans 6:4 to the biblical narratives of crossing the Red Sea and the Jordan River, we witnessed how full immersion baptism aligns with the timeless themes of death and resurrection.

The practical aspects of full immersion unveiled meticulous preparations and ceremonies that underscore the solemnity of this act. From the filling of the baptismal pool to the role of baptizers as spiritual guides, we recognized that even the most practical details are infused with spiritual significance. This practicality is a testament to the intentionality and reverence that surround full immersion baptism.

Ceremonially, full immersion baptism is a masterpiece of symbolism. It echoes the burial and resurrection of Christ, serving as a tangible reminder of the believer's journey from sin to redemption. Personal testimonials, like Victoria's, bore witness to the transformative power of this symbolic journey, demonstrating that full immersion is not just an ancient ritual but a living testament to the ongoing transformation that faith in Christ brings.

As we conclude this chapter, we leave the baptismal waters with a profound appreciation for the act and art of full immersion. It is an artistry that transcends time and culture, a deeply spiritual act that bridges theology and practice, and a journey that forever alters the lives of those who undertake it.

In the chapters ahead, we will continue to explore the transformative act of water baptism, uncovering its contemporary relevance, its symbolism, and the stories of those who have been forever changed by these sacred waters.

CHAPTER SIX

The Debate Unfolds: Salvation and the Role of Water Baptism

"There is one body and one Spirit—just as you were called to the one
hope that belongs to your call—one Lord, one faith, one baptism."
—EPHESIANS 4:4–5 ESV

Within the intricate tapestry of Christian theology, there
exists a profound and enduring debate—a debate that
has captivated the hearts and minds of theologians, pastors,
and believers for centuries. This debate centers on the
relationship between water baptism and salvation, two pillars
of the Christian faith that have been sources of deep
contemplation, spirited discourse, and divergent viewpoints.

As we venture into the heart of this theological tempest, we find ourselves on a quest for understanding, a journey that will illuminate the rich landscape of Christian thought on this intricate matter.

The question at the heart of this debate is one of profound significance: Does water baptism play a role in the salvation of the believer, and if so, what is the nature of that role?

The divergent answers to this question have given rise to a spectrum of theological perspectives within the Christian tradition. Some argue that baptism is a sacramental act that imparts grace and regeneration, an essential component in the process of salvation. Others maintain that while baptism holds importance as an act of obedience and identification with Christ, salvation is ultimately dependent on faith alone.

This chapter embarks on a journey through the theological landscapes that encompass these differing viewpoints, exploring the scriptural foundations, historical developments, and contemporary reflections that have shaped the discussion. The scriptural passages that have fueled this debate are numerous and multifaceted. Mark 16:16 presents a direct connection between belief and baptism for salvation, while Acts 2:38 associates repentance and baptism with the forgiveness of sins.

Yet, equally significant are passages that emphasize faith as the central element of salvation, such as Romans 10:9, which declares that "if you confess with your mouth that Jesus is Lord and believe in your heart that God raised him from the dead, you will be saved." As we explore these scriptures, we tread upon sacred ground, seeking to unravel their profound implications and the varying interpretations they have inspired.

This theological debate has not only enriched Christian discourse but has also been a source of historical controversies that have left an indelible mark on Christian doctrine and practice. The centuries-old dispute between proponents of infant baptism and believers' baptism, with its roots in differing interpretations of scripture, has given rise to distinct theological traditions within Christianity. Additionally, the debate over the mode of baptism—full immersion, pouring, or sprinkling—continues to shape liturgical practices and denominational distinctives.

While historical divisions and theological debates endure, the Christian faith is also marked by a spirit of reconciliation and unity. Contemporary theologians and denominations are engaging in thoughtful dialogues, seeking to bridge theological gaps and emphasize the common ground that unites believers in their shared faith in Christ. Ecumenical efforts and interdenominational discussions are fostering a sense of unity within the diverse body of Christ, guided by the prayer of Jesus in John 17:21, which fervently implores for the unity of all believers.

As we journey through this chapter, we recognize that the debate over water baptism and salvation is not merely a theological discussion but a reflection of the ongoing quest for understanding and unity within the Christian faith. It is a debate that encapsulates the richness of Christian thought, the depth of scriptural exploration, and the enduring commitment of believers to seek truth and unity in the face of theological diversity.

Baptism and Salvation in Christian Theology

In the tapestry of Christian theology, few threads are as intricate and debated as the connection between water baptism and salvation. As we embark on the first topic of this chapter, we delve into the rich tapestry of theological perspectives that have shaped the understanding of how baptism relates to the profound concept of salvation. To navigate these theological waters, we'll explore various interpretations of key biblical passages and the spirited debates that have unfolded over time, all with the aim of shedding light on the role of baptism in the grand narrative of salvation.

One pivotal biblical passage that has ignited theological discussions is Mark 16:16, where Jesus Himself declares, "Whoever believes and is baptized will be saved, but whoever does not believe will be condemned." This verse, often cited in discussions about baptism and salvation, suggests a direct connection between faith, baptism, and salvation. However, interpretations vary widely, with some emphasizing the necessity of baptism for salvation, while others focus on faith as the primary catalyst for salvation.

Another scripture that has been central to this debate is Acts 2:38, where Peter exhorts his audience to "Repent and be baptized, every one of you, in the name of Jesus Christ for the forgiveness of your sins." This passage raises questions about whether baptism is a requirement for the forgiveness of sins or an outward expression of repentance and faith.

The theological debates surrounding these passages and others have given rise to diverse perspectives within Christianity. Some traditions hold that baptism is a sacrament that imparts grace and regeneration, playing a central role in the process of salvation. Others view it as an important but not salvific act, emphasizing faith as the sole means of salvation. These varying theological perspectives have influenced doctrinal formulations, worship practices, and denominational identities within the Christian faith.

As we navigate this complex terrain of theology, it becomes clear that the relationship between water baptism and salvation is a topic steeped in deep convictions and thoughtful reflection. This chapter seeks to illuminate these varied perspectives, acknowledging that within the rich tapestry of Christian thought, different threads contribute to a diverse yet unified understanding of the transformative act of water baptism and its role in the tapestry of salvation.

Ripples of Faith: Exploring the Role of
Baptism in Salvation

In the bustling city of Charleston, South Carolina, Pastor Adam navigated the complexities of his diverse congregation at Grace Community Church. Known for his gentle demeanor and insightful teachings, he found himself at the center of a theological debate that stirred passionate discussions among his church members: the role of baptism in salvation.

Pastor Adam decided to address the topic in a series of sermons, hoping to illuminate the rich tapestry of theological perspectives within Christianity and foster understanding among his congregation. Each Sunday, he introduced key biblical passages that sparked the debate, such as Mark 16:16 and Acts 2:38, and explored their interpretations.

One Sunday, he focused on Thomas, a church elder who had grown up believing that baptism was essential for salvation. Thomas shared his journey, recounting a childhood marked by strict religious adherence and a profound respect for the sacraments. His testimony revealed how his views had evolved over time, especially after his studies in theology. He now viewed baptism more as a powerful symbol of entering into the Christian faith, an outward expression of an inward grace, rather than a requirement for salvation.

The following week, Pastor Adam introduced Sarah, a recent convert whose understanding of baptism was shaped by her experience at a community baptism event. Sarah described how, upon her decision to follow Christ, she felt an urgent need to be baptized. For her, the act of being submerged and rising out of the water was a transformative experience that signified her new life and cleansing from past sins. For Sarah, baptism felt like an integral part of her salvation experience, a moment where she felt deeply connected to Christ's death and resurrection.

Each story stirred the congregation, bringing to light the personal and communal aspects of baptism. Pastor Adam used these narratives to demonstrate how diverse experiences and interpretations can coexist within the same faith community. He emphasized that while theological perspectives might vary, the essential truth remains—baptism is a profound step in the Christian journey, rich with symbolic meaning and capable of touching hearts deeply.

As the sermon series concluded, Pastor Adam encouraged his congregation to respect and embrace their differences, reminding them of the unity they shared in Christ. He quoted Ephesians 4:5, "One Lord, one faith, one baptism," to highlight that despite diverse views, they were all part of one body, united by their faith and the transformative journey of following Jesus.

The value of these discussions and testimonies lay not just in theological education but in the way they enriched the congregation's fellowship and mutual understanding. They learned that each believer's journey was unique yet bound by common threads of faith, baptism, and the ongoing transformation in Christ.

━━━━━━

Historical Controversies and Debates

As we continue our journey through the theological currents of water baptism and salvation, we now plunge into the tempestuous waters of historical controversies and debates. These debates, like roaring waves crashing against the shores of Christian tradition, have left a profound impact on how the relationship between baptism and salvation is understood. In this second topic, we will explore the notable theological conflicts that have emerged over the centuries, shedding light on how these controversies have sculpted the contours of Christian doctrine.

One of the most enduring and contentious debates has been the dispute between proponents of infant baptism and those who advocate for believers' baptism. The crux of this debate revolves around the question of when an individual should be baptized: in infancy or upon a confession of faith. This theological tussle finds its roots in differing interpretations of biblical passages, such as Acts 8:12, which records the baptisms of believers, and Acts 16:33, where an entire household is baptized. The debate has led to the formation of distinct theological traditions within Christianity, each emphasizing its own understanding of baptism's relationship to salvation.

Another historical controversy that has left a lasting imprint is the debate over the mode of baptism. Should it be performed through full immersion, pouring, or sprinkling? This question, though seemingly practical, carries theological weight as it touches on the symbolism and significance of baptism. Scripture provides glimpses into these practices, with the Apostle Paul describing baptism as a burial and resurrection in Romans 6:4, while Hebrews 10:22 speaks of "having our hearts sprinkled clean from an evil conscience." These diverse scriptural references have fueled debates, leading to variations in baptismal practices among Christian denominations.

These historical controversies and debates have not only shaped the way baptism is practiced but also influenced broader Christian doctrines and traditions. They have contributed to denominational divisions, theological distinctives, and liturgical practices. While the debates may persist, they underscore the richness of Christian thought and the enduring significance of baptism within the diverse tapestry of the faith.

As we sail through these historical waters of contention, we gain insight into the passionate discussions and differing viewpoints that have marked the Christian journey. The debates, though tumultuous, remind us of the vitality of theological exploration and the enduring quest to understand the transformative act of water baptism within the context of salvation.

Debates and Divinity: Exploring Historical Controversies on Baptism and Salvation

In the academic halls of a distinguished theological seminary, Dr. Martin Voss, a professor with decades of experience in Church history, prepares to lead a seminar that delves into the historical controversies surrounding baptism and its theological implications for salvation. The classroom is filled with students from various denominational backgrounds, each bringing their unique perspectives to the table.

As Dr. Voss introduces the topic, he outlines the key historical debates that have shaped Christian doctrine over the centuries, particularly focusing on the contentious issues of infant versus believers' baptism and the mode of baptism—full immersion, pouring, or sprinkling. His deep knowledge and engaging teaching style captivate the students, who are eager to explore how these theological battles have sculpted the contours of their faith traditions.

The first major discussion point in the seminar is the debate over infant baptism versus believers' baptism. Dr. Voss explains how this debate centers on the interpretation of scripture passages such as Acts 8:12 and Acts 16:33. He challenges the students to consider the implications of baptizing infants who are not yet capable of professing faith versus waiting until an individual can make a personal confession of faith.

To deepen their understanding, Dr. Voss assigns a group project. Each group must research and present how their respective denominations have interpreted these scriptures and how these interpretations have influenced their baptismal practices. The groups are mixed, encouraging students from different backgrounds to collaborate and understand each other's viewpoints.

As the seminar progresses, Dr. Voss shifts focus to the debate over the mode of baptism. He highlights how Romans 6:4 and Hebrews 10:22 have been pivotal in shaping doctrinal stances on whether baptism should be performed by full immersion, which symbolizes burial and resurrection, or by sprinkling, seen as a cleansing from sins. The discussion becomes particularly animated as students share personal experiences and doctrinal teachings from their communities.

In the final weeks of the seminar, Dr. Voss organizes a panel discussion with local church leaders from various denominations to discuss the current state of ecumenical efforts towards unity despite these long-standing differences. This event not only enriches the students' understanding but also inspires them to appreciate the diversity within the body of Christ.

The seminar concludes with students reflecting on how their own views have been challenged and expanded. They express a newfound appreciation for the depth and complexity of Christian doctrine and a greater respect for traditions other than their own. Dr. Voss, pleased with the vigorous engagement and thoughtful discourse, notes that while the debates may persist, they serve as a testament to the vitality of theological exploration and the shared commitment to understanding the profound elements of their faith.

Through this academic journey, the students not only gain academic knowledge but also develop a deeper spiritual maturity, recognizing that their exploration of baptism's historical controversies is not just an intellectual exercise but a meaningful endeavor that connects them more deeply to their faith and to each other.

═══════

Contemporary Perspectives and Reconciliation

In the ever-evolving landscape of Christian theology, the debate over the relationship between water baptism and salvation continues to stir the waters. However, in this final topic of Chapter 6, we turn our gaze toward the shores of reconciliation and unity within the diverse body of Christ. As we navigate contemporary perspectives on this age-old debate, we discover how theologians and denominations are striving to bridge theological gaps, emphasizing the common ground that unites believers in their shared faith.

Contemporary theologians, like skilled navigators on the sea of theological discourse, have sought to foster a sense of unity within the Christian community by acknowledging the richness of differing perspectives on baptism and salvation. They emphasize that, while differences persist, there is a shared confession of faith in Christ that transcends denominational boundaries. This unity is beautifully encapsulated in Ephesians 4:5, which reminds us, "One Lord, one faith, one baptism."

One approach to reconciliation involves recognizing that the relationship between baptism and salvation is multifaceted, accommodating a spectrum of theological viewpoints. Some contemporary theologians advocate for a balanced perspective, highlighting the significance of both faith and baptism in the Christian journey. They argue that faith is the primary catalyst for salvation, but baptism serves as a tangible expression and affirmation of that faith. This perspective draws from biblical passages such as Acts 22:16, where baptism is linked to the washing away of sins and calling on the name of the Lord.

Moreover, interdenominational dialogue and ecumenical efforts have gained momentum in recent years. These initiatives bring together representatives from various Christian traditions to engage in thoughtful and respectful discussions on topics like baptism and salvation. The aim is not to eliminate differences but to foster understanding and unity within the diverse body of Christ. This approach aligns with the prayer of Jesus in John 17:21, where He fervently prays for the unity of all believers.

Denominations, too, have shown a willingness to engage in ecumenical dialogue and emphasize shared beliefs. While differences in baptismal theology persist, there is a growing recognition that the Christian faith is a unifying force that transcends doctrinal distinctions. This recognition encourages believers to focus on the essentials of their faith and the transformative power of their shared commitment to Christ.

In contemporary times, the theological debates surrounding baptism and salvation remain a dynamic part of Christian discourse. However, a spirit of reconciliation and unity is breathing life into these discussions. As Christians navigate the theological currents, they are reminded that, regardless of their theological perspectives, they are bound together by a common faith in Christ, a faith that calls them to love and unity, for, as Romans 15:7 proclaims, "Therefore welcome one another as Christ has welcomed you, for the glory of God."

Unity Amid Diversity: Bridging Theological Divides in Modern Christianity

In the bustling cityscape of Philadelphia, a unique gathering unfolds within the historic walls of Trinity Chapel—a symposium titled "Baptism and Salvation: A Dialogue for Unity." Here, theologians, pastors, and laypeople from a wide array of Christian denominations come together, each bringing a diverse tapestry of beliefs centered around the themes of baptism and salvation.

Among the attendees is Esau, a theologian with a gentle demeanor and a deep passion for ecumenism. He has spent years studying various theological perspectives, driven by a belief that the heart of Christian unity beats strongest when embracing diversity. Esau is particularly intrigued by how different denominations interpret the role of baptism in salvation—some viewing it as essential for salvation, others as a symbolic affirmation of faith.

As the symposium begins, Esau listens intently to the opening remarks, which emphasize a shared commitment to Christ's teachings as the foundation for unity. The keynote speaker, Dr. Lydia Hanson, a renowned theologian known for her work on interdenominational dialogue, cites Ephesians 4:5, "One Lord, one faith, one baptism," underscoring the shared confession that binds all Christians.

The first panel discussion, "The Sacramental View of Baptism," features speakers from Catholic, Orthodox, and Lutheran backgrounds. They discuss how baptism, in their traditions, is seen as a conduit of divine grace and an initiation into the Christian faith. Each speaker presents their doctrinal views with respect and clarity, highlighting the sacramental nature of baptism as a profound encounter with God's grace.

Esau participates in the second panel, "Baptism as Symbolic Obedience." Joined by representatives from Baptist and evangelical communities, the discussion revolves around the concept of believer's baptism—performed upon confession of faith, emphasizing baptism as a public declaration of faith and discipleship. Esau presents his perspective that while faith alone is central to salvation, baptism is a vital act of obedience and public testimony.

Throughout the discussions, the floor is open for questions and reflections from the audience, facilitating a respectful and enriching exchange of ideas. The atmosphere, though charged with diverse opinions, is marked by a mutual respect and a common desire to understand one another's viewpoints.

One poignant moment comes when a young pastor from a non-denominational church shares her experience of witnessing baptisms in her community. She speaks about the transformative power she has observed in the lives of those baptized, regardless of the theological nuances discussed. Her testimony reminds everyone of the practical impact of these theological concepts on everyday faith.

As the symposium draws to a close, Esau reflects on the journey of the day. He feels a renewed hope that such dialogues can bridge the gaps between Christian traditions. The closing prayer, echoing Jesus's desire for unity among His followers, leaves a powerful impression on all present.

In the weeks following the symposium, Esau pens an article for a theological journal, titled "Unity in Diversity: The Ecumenical Journey of Baptism and Salvation." He writes about the experiences shared, the insights gained, and the common faith that unites all participants. His story serves as a beacon of hope, illustrating that even in a landscape marked by theological diversity, there is a path forward together, guided by a commitment to understanding, respect, and shared faith in Christ.

———

Conclusion

As we draw the curtains on Chapter 6, "The Debate Unfolds: Salvation and the Role of Water Baptism," we find ourselves on the shores of a profound and enduring theological conversation—one that has animated the hearts and minds of Christians across the centuries. The relationship between water baptism and salvation, this theological tempest, has continued to challenge and enrich our understanding of the Christian faith.

Throughout this chapter, we navigated the theological currents, exploring the rich tapestry of perspectives on this intricate matter. From those who emphasize the sacramental nature of baptism as a means of grace to those who uphold faith as the central element of salvation, we encountered the diversity of thought that defines the Christian tradition.

In our quest for understanding, we ventured into scriptural passages that have fueled the debate, discovering that the Bible presents a multifaceted view of baptism's role in the Christian journey. We traced the historical controversies, such as the age-old debate between infant baptism and believers' baptism, and the intricacies of the mode of baptism, which continue to shape Christian traditions.

Yet, even as this theological discourse has been marked by divisions and debates, it is also a testament to the enduring commitment of Christians to seek unity within the diverse body of Christ. Contemporary theologians, denominations, and ecumenical efforts have sought to bridge theological gaps and emphasize the common faith that unites believers. In this spirit, they echo the words of the Apostle Paul in Ephesians 4:5, recognizing the unifying confession of "One Lord, one faith, one baptism."

As we close this chapter, we do so with an appreciation for the richness of Christian thought and the enduring quest for understanding within the faith. The debate over water baptism and salvation, with its diverse viewpoints and historical controversies, reminds us that the Christian journey is marked by both theological diversity and a shared commitment to Christ. It underscores that, regardless of our differences, we are united in our faith, our pursuit of truth, and our call to love one another. In the chapters that lie ahead, we will continue to explore the transformative act of water baptism, examining its contemporary relevance, its profound symbolism, and the stories of those whose lives have been forever changed by these sacred waters.

CHAPTER SEVEN

Post-Baptismal Awakening: The Immediate Aftermath of the Act

"Instead, speaking the truth in love, we will grow to become in every respect the mature body of him who is the head, that is, Christ. From him the whole body, joined and held together by every supporting ligament, grows and builds itself up in love, as each part does its work."

—EPHESIANS 4:15–16 NIV

In the serene moments following the sacred act of water baptism, a profound transformation unfolds—a transformation that extends far beyond the waters themselves. As we step into Chapter 7, we find ourselves in the realm of post-baptismal awakening, a captivating journey that explores the immediate impact of baptism on individuals and their integration into the vibrant tapestry of the faith community.

Baptism is not merely a solitary event; it is a communal celebration, a declaration that echoes throughout the lives of those who have taken the plunge. In these sacred moments, individuals often describe a profound sense of cleansing, renewal, and spiritual awakening—a rekindling of the divine flame within. These are the stories that grace our path, stories that resonate with the timeless truth of Psalm 51:10, "Create in me a clean heart, O God, and renew a right spirit within me."

But the journey does not end at the baptismal font. It is merely the beginning of an extraordinary voyage—a voyage that leads individuals into the embrace of a faith community. The church, like a lighthouse guiding ships safely to shore, plays a pivotal role in nurturing and supporting the newly baptized, helping them find their place within the congregation. It is a place where faith becomes not just personal but communal, a shared journey where believers walk alongside one another in the pursuit of Christ's teachings.

Yet, this chapter also acknowledges that the post-baptismal journey can be marked by challenges and questions. Doubts may surface, uncertainties may linger, and the newly baptized may find themselves navigating uncharted spiritual waters. However, it is within these moments of uncertainty that faith has the opportunity to deepen and mature. It is a reminder that faith is not static but dynamic, a living relationship with our Creator.

As we delve into Chapter 7, we embark on a profound exploration of the immediate aftermath of baptism—an exploration that captures the essence of spiritual awakening, community integration, and the challenges that shape our faith. This is a chapter of stories, questions, and discoveries—a chapter that unveils the transformative power of baptism in the lives of those who dare to embrace its sacred waters.

The Spiritual Impact of Baptism

In the serene moments that follow the immersion into the baptismal waters, something remarkable occurs—a spiritual awakening that ignites the hearts of the newly baptized. Like a gentle breeze that rustles the leaves of a dormant tree, baptism breathes new life into the soul. This profound spiritual impact is often described as a sense of cleansing, renewal, and awakening—a rekindling of the divine flame within. It echoes the words of Psalm 51:10, "Create in me a clean heart, O God, and renew a right spirit within me."

For those who have taken this transformative plunge, personal testimonials resound with a common refrain: a profound sense of being cleansed from the stains of the past. Baptism, in its sacred waters, washes away the weight of sins and transgressions, leaving behind a soul that feels lighter, purer, and more intimately connected to the Divine. This sense of cleansing is not just a metaphorical abstraction; it is a tangible experience, a spiritual shower that refreshes the spirit. In Acts 22:16, the Apostle Paul, recounting his own baptism, emphasizes how baptism is linked to the washing away of sins, a truth that resonates deeply with many.

But it doesn't end there. Baptism also ushers in a profound sense of renewal, akin to the rebirth of nature in the springtime. It marks a fresh start, a clean slate upon which the story of faith can be rewritten. The Apostle Paul captures this renewal beautifully in 2 Corinthians 5:17, declaring, "Therefore, if anyone is in Christ, he is a new creation. The old has passed away; behold, the new has come." This renewal often manifests in a newfound zeal for living out the teachings of Christ, an invigorated commitment to love, serve, and follow the path of righteousness.

As we explore the spiritual impact of baptism, we encounter personal stories that bear witness to the transformation that occurs in these sacred moments. Believers, old and young, recount how their baptism became a turning point—a catalyst for a deeper, more vibrant connection to faith. Their testimonials, like radiant stars in the night sky, illuminate the spiritual awakening that baptism kindles within the soul. These stories serve as a testament to the enduring power of this ancient ritual and remind us that, indeed, "baptism . . . now saves you, not as a removal of dirt from the body but as an appeal to God for a good conscience, through the resurrection of Jesus Christ" (1 Peter 3:21).

Renewed by the River: Gideon's Journey
of Baptismal Transformation

In the tranquil village of Maplebrook, the story of Gideon—a humble carpenter known for his kindness and quiet strength—illustrates the profound spiritual impact of baptism vividly. Gideon had lived a life marked by hardship and personal failure, often feeling as if he were adrift in a sea of regrets. His past was littered with broken promises and missed opportunities, casting a long shadow over his present.

One bright spring morning, Gideon made his way to the local church, drawn by a yearning for renewal and a whisper of hope that had begun to stir within his heart. As he stood on the banks of the river behind the church, watching others emerge from the water with faces alight with joy, Gideon felt a deep pull in his soul. Encouraged by the pastor, he decided to take the step he had long postponed.

With the congregation gathered around, singing hymns of redemption, Gideon stepped into the cold, flowing river. The water closed over him, and in that submerged moment, a profound sense of peace washed over him. As he rose from the river, the weight of his past seemed to dissolve into the water, leaving him feeling lighter and startlingly new. The stains of his former life, the guilt and the regret, seemed to remain beneath the surface, washed away by the grace of the moment.

Gideon's baptism marked the beginning of a remarkable transformation. He found himself infused with a new energy and purpose, approaching his craft with greater passion and treating his neighbors with deeper kindness. The spiritual renewal he experienced was not confined to his personal feelings; it was evident in his actions and interactions. He began volunteering at the church, helping to repair old structures and building furniture for families in need. His life became a living testament to the renewal he had experienced, embodying the scripture, "Therefore, if anyone is in Christ, he is a new creation. The old has passed away; behold, the new has come."

As the seasons changed in Maplebrook, Gideon's journey of faith deepened. He became a pillar in the community, a beacon of hope and transformation. His story spread beyond the village, drawing others to seek out this powerful renewal for themselves. Through his experience, the spiritual impact of baptism shone brightly—a tangible demonstration of an internal and external transformation, inspiring a community and rekindling the divine flame within many hearts.

———

Baptism and Community Integration

The ripple effect of baptism extends far beyond the moment when water touches skin and soul. It is a transformation not meant to be solitary but communal, an invitation to become a vital part of the faith family. In the immediate aftermath of baptism, individuals often find themselves at the threshold of a new spiritual home—a community of believers ready to embrace them, nurture their faith, and walk alongside them in their journey.

The church, like a welcoming harbor for weary travelers, plays a pivotal role in this integration process. It is a place where the newly baptized find not just a congregation but a spiritual family—a community bound together by a shared commitment to follow Christ. In Ephesians 2:19–22, the Apostle Paul beautifully describes this sense of belonging, proclaiming, "So then you are no longer strangers and aliens, but you are fellow citizens with the saints and members of the household of God."

Baptism, in a profound way, marks the initiation into this household, a sacred adoption into the family of faith. Within the faith community, there exists a nurturing spirit, akin to that of a gardener tending to fragile seedlings. It is a collective effort to ensure that the newly baptized are provided with the spiritual sustenance they need to grow in their faith. Encouragement, discipleship, and mentorship become essential components of this journey, reminiscent of Paul's guidance in Galatians 6:2, "Bear one another's burdens, and so fulfill the law of Christ."

Fellow believers, like co-travelers on a pilgrim's path, play a significant role in the integration of the newly baptized. Their support and fellowship become sources of strength and encouragement. They provide the camaraderie that reminds the newly baptized that they are not alone on this journey. In

Hebrews 10:24–25, believers are urged to "consider how to stir up one another to love and good works, not neglecting to meet together." Baptism becomes the gateway to this ongoing fellowship, where believers gather, not just as individuals but as a collective body, to worship, learn, and grow in their faith.

In the immediate aftermath of baptism, individuals step into a new chapter of their faith journey—one marked by the warmth of community, the support of fellow believers, and the nurturing embrace of the church. It is a chapter where the words of Jesus in John 13:35 find vivid expression: "By this all people will know that you are my disciples if you have love for one another." Baptism, in its profound way, affirms and deepens this love within the Christian community, making it a place of refuge, growth, and spiritual enrichment for all who embark on this transformative journey.

A New Family in Faith: Ezekiel's Journey of Integration After Baptism

Ezekiel stood on the shores of transformation, his clothes still dripping from the baptismal waters. His heart, freshly washed by the act of baptism, felt lighter, and the sense of being part of something greater than himself was overwhelming. For years, Ezekiel had wandered through life without a spiritual anchor, his days filled with routine and his relationships superficial at best. But this day marked a new beginning.

As he stepped out of the water, he was not stepping back into his old life, but forward into a community—a family bound by faith. The church that had once seemed just a structure of wood and stone now felt like a home, vibrant with the spirit of companionship and mutual commitment to follow Christ.

In the weeks that followed, the integration into his new faith family was both exhilarating and challenging. Each handshake and hug from fellow congregants was a stitch weaving him into the tapestry of the community. The church's role as a nurturing harbor became evident as he was invited to join various groups within the church. Bible studies, volunteer opportunities, and fellowship dinners—they all played their parts in knitting Ezekiel's life into the larger fabric of the congregation.

Ephesians 2:19–22 echoed profoundly within him, transforming the text from mere words to a living reality. "So then you are no longer strangers and aliens, but you are fellow citizens with the saints and members of the household of God," the pastor had quoted during his first service after the baptism. This verse became a daily affirmation for Ezekiel, reminding him of his new identity and belonging.

The faith community, recognizing their role in nurturing Ezekiel's newfound spiritual awakening, embraced him wholeheartedly. Seasoned members of the church became mentors, echoing Galatians 6:2, as they shared their experiences and wisdom, helping him bear the burdens of his past and the uncertainties of his new journey.

Hebrews 10:24-25 became a call to action for Ezekiel and his fellow believers, encouraging one another to love and good works. The church gatherings became more than rituals; they were reunions of a family eager to support one another in faith and action.

The transformation was not without its challenges. Doubts whispered at the edges of his thoughts, and old habits tugged at his resolve. But the community stood by him, their actions and support a constant reminder of the shared journey of faith they all walked. It was in these moments of vulnerability that the words of John 13:35 shone the brightest: "By this all people will know that you are my disciples, if you have love for one another."

Ezekiel's baptism marked not the conclusion of a spiritual quest but the commencement of a life rich in community and faith. With each passing day, the ripple effects of that moment by the baptismal waters continued to expand, touching every aspect of his life and reinforcing the profound truth that in this family of believers, he was no longer a stranger but a beloved brother. The warmth of this community, the strength of their shared faith, and the depth of their collective love were the true hallmarks of his post-baptismal awakening—a testament to the transformative power of baptism in the life of a believer.

Challenges and Questions After Baptism

Baptism, a sacred and transformative act, often marks the beginning of a remarkable spiritual journey, yet it does not guarantee immunity from challenges and questions. In the wake of the waters, as the ripples of transformation spread, individuals may find themselves navigating uncharted territory, wrestling with doubts and uncertainties that accompany their newfound faith. However, it is precisely within these moments of uncertainty that faith has the opportunity to deepen and mature.

It is not uncommon for individuals, in the wake of their baptism, to grapple with questions. Doubts may surface like unexpected waves, and uncertainties may loom like dark clouds on a clear day. These moments are not signs of faith's weakness but rather its potential for growth. The Apostle James, in James 1:6, encourages us to approach these challenges with faith, declaring, "But let him ask in faith, with no doubting, for the one who doubts is like a wave of the sea that is driven and tossed by the wind."

Some common questions may include pondering the nature of God, seeking to understand His will, and grappling with the complexities of faith. These questions, rather than being feared, should be embraced as opportunities for spiritual growth and maturation. As we seek answers, we are reminded of Proverbs 2:3–5, which assures us, "Yes, if you call out for insight and raise your voice for understanding, if you seek it like silver and search for it as for hidden treasures, then you will understand the fear of the Lord and find the knowledge of God."

Nurturing faith in the face of challenges often involves seeking guidance and support within the faith community. This is where the importance of ongoing discipleship and spiritual growth becomes paramount. Encouragement from fellow believers, the wisdom of mentors, and the nourishment of the Word of God all play crucial roles in navigating the post-baptismal journey. The Psalmist captures this beautifully in Psalm 119:105, proclaiming, "Your word is a lamp to my feet and a light to my path."

Stella's Journey Through Doubt and Discovery

After the serene waters of her baptism settled, Stella stood at the threshold of a new spiritual dawn. The ceremony had been everything she dreamed—full of hope, community, and sacred promises. Yet, as the days unfolded, the euphoria waned, and in its place, questions began to seep through the cracks of her newly formed faith.

Stella, a young graphic designer, had always prided herself on her analytical mind, which served her well in her profession but now posed challenging questions about her faith. "What is God's plan for me?" "How can I reconcile my faith with the doubts that keep surfacing?" These were not questions of rebellion but of a deep desire to understand and integrate her faith more fully into her life.

As doubts surfaced like unexpected waves, threatening to toss her newfound faith, Stella recalled the words of James 1:6, encouraging believers to ask in faith without doubting. Motivated by this, she turned to her church's community, seeking not just answers but a deeper connection with her faith.

Stella's journey through doubt was not a solitary struggle. She found solace and support in a small Bible study group, where she met Nathan, an older church member known for his wisdom and understanding of the scriptures. Nathan became a mentor to Stella, guiding her through her doubts with patience and insight. Their sessions often revolved around deep discussions, where Proverbs 2:3–5 was a recurring theme, encouraging Stella to seek wisdom as a hidden treasure.

One evening, during a particularly challenging discussion, Nathan shared Psalm 119:105, explaining, "Your word is a lamp to my feet and a light to my path." This verse struck a chord with Stella, illuminating her understanding that her journey was not about having all the answers but about walking in faith, guided by the light of God's Word.

The support from Nathan and her community did not erase Stella's doubts overnight, but it provided her with the tools and the confidence to navigate them. She learned that faith was not static but dynamic, involving an ongoing dialogue with God and the community.

Over time, Stella's faith matured. She began to see her doubts not as obstacles but as avenues for growth and deeper understanding. Her journey became one of continuous discovery, where each question led to deeper insights and a stronger, more resilient faith.

Through her post-baptismal challenges, Stella realized that her faith was like a tree, rooted in the rich soil of her community and nourished by the waters of baptism. It was a living, breathing entity that grew stronger through the storms of doubt and the sunshine of understanding.

Stella's story, from the transformative waters of baptism to the ongoing journey of faith, serves as a testament to the power of community and the enduring grace of spiritual growth. It reminds us all that the path of faith is not marked by the absence of doubt but by our response to it, guided by the lamp of God's Word and the fellowship of believers.

––––––––––

Conclusion

As we conclude our exploration of Chapter 7, "Post-Baptismal Awakening: The Immediate Aftermath of the Act," we find ourselves at the threshold of an inspiring and transformative journey—a journey that extends far beyond the baptismal font. In these sacred moments, individuals often encounter a profound spiritual awakening, a sense of renewal, and a cleansing of the soul that beckons them toward a deeper connection with the Divine.

This awakening, as we have discovered, is not meant to be a solitary experience. It is an invitation to become an integral part of a faith community, a spiritual family that offers warmth, support, and nourishment to the newly baptized. The church, like a steadfast anchor in the stormy seas of life, plays a vital role in nurturing and guiding believers on their faith journey.

Yet, our exploration did not shy away from acknowledging the challenges and questions that often follow baptism. Doubts may arise, uncertainties may linger, but these moments are not indicative of a faith weakened; rather, they are opportunities for faith to grow, deepen, and mature. It is in these moments of questioning that we are reminded of the enduring power of faith—a power that propels us forward in our spiritual pilgrimage.

In the grand tapestry of faith, baptism marks the beginning of an extraordinary voyage—a voyage filled with moments of cleansing, renewal, community, and introspection. It is a journey of stories and questions, of doubts and discoveries. It is a journey where faith is not a stagnant pond but a flowing river, where spiritual awakening, community integration, and the challenges that shape our faith converge.

As we step away from Chapter 7, we carry with us the profound truth that baptism is not just a one-time event but a lifelong commitment—a commitment to continue growing, learning, and discovering the depths of our faith. It is a commitment to walk alongside fellow believers, drawing strength from one another, and to seek answers to our questions, knowing that in our pursuit, we draw closer to the heart of God.

The post-baptismal journey is a testament to the enduring power of faith—a journey marked by the transformative waters of baptism, the warmth of community, and the resilience of the human spirit. In the chapters that lie ahead, we will continue to explore the multifaceted nature of water baptism, uncovering its timeless significance and the myriad ways it shapes our lives as believers.

CHAPTER EIGHT

Integrating the Rite: Baptism's Place in the Believer's Walk

"Being confident of this, that he who began a good work in you will carry
it on to completion until the day of Christ Jesus."
—PHILIPPIANS 1:6 NIV

In the journey of faith, baptism marks not the end of a story but a breathtaking beginning—a prologue to a life drenched in grace and destined for transformation. As we venture into Chapter 8, we uncover a remarkable truth: baptism is not a solitary event but a catalyst for ongoing spiritual growth. It is the compass that continually guides us on the path of becoming more like Christ.

In this chapter, we explore three profound aspects of baptism's place in the believer's walk. First, we delve into the idea that baptism is a milestone, not a mere moment. It is the marker on our journey of faith, reminding us that the Christian walk is not a sprint but a marathon.

Secondly, we examine the role of baptism in the process of spiritual formation, understanding how it shapes our character, values, and daily spiritual practices.

Finally, we bear witness to the transformative power of baptism through personal stories and testimonials. We listen to voices of those who have experienced remarkable personal changes, mending brokenness, healing relationships, and finding hope in the waters of baptism.

This chapter is a profound exploration of the enduring impact of baptism—a journey of becoming, growing, and embracing the transformative grace of God. As we step into its depths, we are invited to reflect on our own journey, to seek spiritual formation, and to discover the enduring power of personal transformation.

Join us in the discovery of the beautiful interplay between baptism and the believer's walk—a journey marked by grace, purpose, and a continual striving to become more like the One in whose name we were baptized.

Baptism as a Milestone in the Faith Journey

Baptism, as we've come to understand, is not a mere ceremonial act but a profound milestone in the believer's walk with Christ. It is not the final destination but a marker along the path of a lifelong journey of faith. Just as the Israelites marked their journey through the wilderness with stone pillars, so too does baptism mark our passage from the old life to the new. In Romans 6:4, we find the analogy of baptism as a burial and resurrection: "We were buried therefore with him by baptism into death, in order that, just as Christ was raised from the dead by the glory of the Father, we too might walk in newness of life."

Baptism signifies a death to the old self and a rising into a new, transformed life in Christ. As believers, we are called not just to remember our baptism but to reflect on its profound meaning and allow it to serve as a wellspring of spiritual growth and motivation.

Every year on their wedding anniversary, couples often reflect on the commitment they made to one another, renewing their love and dedication. Similarly, our spiritual birthday—the day we were baptized—should be an occasion for reflection and renewal. It's an opportunity to revisit our commitment to follow Christ and to allow the memory of those waters to rekindle our zeal for living out our faith.

Just as the psalmist declares in Psalm 42:1–2, "As a deer pants for flowing streams, so pants my soul for you, O God.

My soul thirsts for God, for the living God," baptism reminds us of the living God to whom we belong and calls us to thirst for a deeper relationship with Him.

Baptism, then, is not a distant memory but a living reality that we carry with us on our journey. It serves as a compass, guiding us toward a life characterized by faith, love, and transformation. It is a marker of our identity as children of God and a source of spiritual motivation as we strive to walk in the footsteps of Christ. In the chapters of life that follow baptism, may we always remember that the waters of baptism were not a destination but a beginning—a beginning of a life drenched in faith and marked by a continual walk with our Savior.

Just as explorers leave markers on their journeys to guide them home, baptism marks us as pilgrims on a spiritual voyage. It reminds us that the path of faith is not a solitary one but a communal journey, and as we walk it, we do so in the company of fellow travelers. The Apostle Paul beautifully articulates this in Galatians 3:26–28, declaring, "for in Christ Jesus you are all sons of God, through faith. For as many of you as were baptized into Christ have put on Christ. There is neither Jew nor Greek, there is neither slave nor free, there is no male and female, for you are all one in Christ Jesus." Baptism unites us in a shared identity as children of God, transcending boundaries and differences.

Reflection on our baptism can also provide a wellspring of motivation in the often-challenging terrain of the believer's walk. Just as athletes draw inspiration from their past victories, we can draw strength from the memory of the waters that marked our initiation into the family of God. In Philippians 3:13–14, the Apostle Paul writes, "Brothers, I do not consider that I have made it my own. But one thing I do: forgetting what lies behind and straining forward to what lies ahead, I press on toward the goal for the prize of the upward call of God in Christ Jesus." Our baptism serves as a reminder of the upward call, urging us to press on in our journey of faith.

In conclusion, baptism is not a momentary event but a milestone, a marker on our lifelong faith journey. It marks us as pilgrims, unites us as a faith community, and motivates us to press on toward the upward call of God. As we reflect on our baptism, may it always remind us of who we are in Christ and inspire us to continue walking the path of faith with unwavering devotion, knowing that our journey is not solitary but shared with fellow believers and guided by the living waters of our baptism.

Rising Waters: Enoch's Journey Through the Ripples of Baptism

Enoch's story begins on a chilly morning that could have been any other day, except it was the day he decided to be baptized. For years, Enoch had wandered through life, often feeling like a ship without a rudder, his moral compass skewed by past regrets and mistakes. Yet, as he stood on the bank of the river that Sunday, he felt an undeniable pull—a call towards a renewal that baptism promised.

As the congregation sang hymns that danced with the morning breeze, Enoch waded into the water, the coldness biting at his ankles, creeping up to wrestle with his resolve. The minister's voice was steady, a beacon as unwavering as the stone pillars the Israelites once raised in the wilderness. When Enoch was submerged, it wasn't just water that enveloped him but a profound sense of dying to an old life, an existence marred by aimlessness and sorrow.

Emerging from the river, Enoch felt the weight of his past sins wash away, not just metaphorically but as a tangible presence lifted from his soul. It was as though he was breathing for the first time, each gulp of air filling him with a newfound purpose. The waters didn't just cleanse; they transformed, rekindling a zeal for life modeled after Christ's teachings.

Reflecting on his baptism became an annual ritual for Enoch, much like a couple renewing their vows. With each year, this reflection didn't just serve as a reminder but as a recommitment to his faith journey—a journey no longer walked in isolation but in the camaraderie of fellow believers. Inspired by the Apostle Paul's words in Philippians, Enoch pressed on, drawing strength from the memory of his baptism, using it as a cornerstone to build a life of faith and service.

The ripple effect of Enoch's baptism reached far beyond his personal transformation. He became an active member of his church, guiding others along their spiritual journeys and helping them recognize their own moments of renewal and commitment. His story became one of many, a testament shared during gatherings, encouraging others to view baptism not just as a ceremony but as a pivotal moment of transformation and communal belonging.

Enoch's baptism was more than a singular event; it was a milestone in a lifelong pilgrimage of faith, a constant reminder of his identity in Christ and a beacon guiding him toward spiritual maturity and collective unity with his faith family. Through baptism, he found not just a community but a family, bound not by blood but by the waters of faith that marked them all as children of God, journeying together towards a divine calling.

The Role of Baptism in Spiritual Formation

Baptism, we have discovered, is not a solitary event but a transformative milestone that continually shapes the believer's walk with Christ. It is a journey that propels us forward on the path of spiritual formation—a process by which our character, values, and spiritual disciplines are molded and refined.

Imagine a potter at the wheel, carefully shaping clay into a vessel of beauty and purpose. Likewise, baptism serves as a moment when the hands of the Divine Potter are upon us, shaping us into vessels of His grace. In 2 Corinthians 3:18, the Apostle Paul reminds us, "And we all, with unveiled face, beholding the glory of the Lord, are being transformed into the same image from one degree of glory to another." Baptism initiates this transformative process, setting us on a trajectory of becoming more like Christ with each passing day.

One of the ways baptism contributes to our spiritual formation is by deepening our awareness of our identity as children of God. It is a declaration to the world that we belong to Christ, and this awareness shapes our character. Just as a mirror reflects our physical appearance, our identity in Christ reflects our spiritual identity. The Apostle Peter writes in 1 Peter 2:9, "But you are a chosen race, a royal priesthood, a holy nation, a people for his own possession, that you may proclaim the excellencies of Him who called you out of darkness into His marvelous light." Baptism reminds us that we are a chosen people, set apart for a holy purpose, and this awareness influences our values and priorities.

Practical integration of baptism's symbolism into our daily lives becomes a natural outflow of this spiritual formation. Just as athletes train rigorously to excel in their sports, we engage in spiritual disciplines to grow in our faith. Baptism inspires us to daily immerse ourselves in prayer, the study of God's Word, and acts of service. It calls us to live out the values of love, forgiveness, and grace, mirroring the life of Christ. The Apostle Paul encourages this in Romans 12:2, saying, "Do not be conformed to this world, but be transformed by the renewal of your mind." Baptism initiates this renewal, and our daily commitment to spiritual disciplines sustains it.

In conclusion, baptism is not a one-time event but a catalyst for ongoing spiritual formation. It shapes our character, values, and spiritual disciplines, inviting us to become vessels of God's grace. As we integrate the symbolism and significance of baptism into our daily lives, we continually reflect the image of Christ and live out our identity as children of God—a journey of profound transformation that unfolds from the waters of baptism into the depths of our faith.

Natalie's Transformation: The Ripple of Baptism

Natalie's spiritual journey took a pivotal turn on a quiet autumn morning, marked by the gentle lapping of river waters at the edge of her small town. As the sun broke through the leaves, casting dappled shadows on the water, Natalie emerged from her baptism, not just cleansed but reborn.

Before her baptism, Natalie struggled with a sense of belonging. Despite years of attending church, she often felt like an outsider looking in, unable to fully grasp her place within the faith community. Baptism changed that. As she rose from the water, it was as if her eyes were opened for the first time to a world filled with color and possibility. The verse from 2 Corinthians 3:18, "We all, with unveiled face, beholding the glory of the Lord, are being transformed into the same image from one degree of glory to another," resonated deeply with her, offering a promise of continual transformation.

This profound moment marked the beginning of Natalie's spiritual formation. With her identity as a child of God reaffirmed, she began to see herself and her world differently. The values she once held began to shift, aligning more closely with those of Christ—values of compassion, patience, and unconditional love.

As part of her ongoing transformation, Natalie integrated the symbolism of her baptism into her daily routine. Each morning, as she prayed, she imagined herself being submerged in the waters of grace, rising refreshed and ready to face the day. She delved into Scripture with renewed vigor, finding in its pages the wisdom to navigate the complexities of life and relationships. Her study of the Word wasn't just an intellectual exercise but a daily feeding of her soul, sustaining her spiritual growth.

Natalie's commitment to living out her baptismal vows led her to serve in her community. She volunteered at a local shelter, extending the hands of Christ to those in need. Each act of service was a reminder of her baptismal call to be a vessel of God's grace. Her transformation was evident to all who knew her; even her moments of doubt and struggle were met with a resilience born of her deepened faith.

The impact of Natalie's baptism rippled through her relationships. Where once there had been friction and estrangement, forgiveness and reconciliation began to flourish. Inspired by Ephesians 4:32, "Be kind to one another, tenderhearted, forgiving one another, as God in Christ forgave you," Natalie reached out to mend old wounds with family and friends, her actions a testament to the transformative power of her faith.

In her faith community, Natalie found not just supporters but fellow pilgrims on the journey of faith. She became involved in discipleship groups, where she both learned and taught, embodying the spirit of mutual edification described in Romans 14:19, "Let us therefore make every effort to do what leads to peace and to mutual edification."

Years later, Natalie stood by the same river where she was baptized, watching others take the same transformative plunge. As she witnessed each baptism, she was reminded of her own spiritual rebirth and the continuous journey of growth it initiated. Her story, a vivid mosaic of personal transformation and communal engagement, served as a beacon to others in her church, inspiring them to embrace the full depth and breadth of their own baptismal journeys.

In conclusion, Natalie's life exemplified the profound truth that baptism is not an endpoint but a gateway to a life of rich spiritual formation. It marked the beginning of her journey of becoming more like Christ, a journey characterized by daily renewal, active service, and deep, lasting change within her community.

———————

Baptism and Personal Transformation

Within the sacred waters of baptism, we find not only a profound declaration of faith but a source of personal transformation that ripples throughout a believer's life. It is a journey that inspires profound changes in the hearts, minds, and actions of those who dare to immerse themselves in its transformative embrace.

Consider the story of Elsa, a young woman whose life was marred by a past filled with regrets and pain. Through the act of baptism, she found not just forgiveness but also the strength to forgive herself. In the forgiving waters, she discovered the powerful truth of 2 Corinthians 5:17, "Therefore, if anyone is in Christ, he is a new creation. The old has passed away; behold, the new has come." Baptism became a catalyst for her personal transformation, a journey from brokenness to wholeness, from despair to hope.

Or consider the testimony of Harry, whose relationships were marred by anger and bitterness. Through the waters of baptism, he experienced the cleansing and healing of his heart. As Ephesians 4:31–32 reminds us, "Let all bitterness and wrath and anger and clamor and slander be put away from you, along with all malice. Be kind to one another, tenderhearted, forgiving one another, as God in Christ forgave you." Baptism ignited a personal transformation within him, leading to restored relationships and a heart filled with grace.

These stories remind us that baptism is not a mere ritual but a life-altering encounter with the living God. It is an encounter that leads to personal growth and sanctification, a journey from darkness to light, from bondage to freedom. The enduring impact of baptism is not confined to the waters but permeates every facet of a believer's life.

Just as a butterfly emerges from the cocoon, forever transformed, so too do individuals emerge from the waters of baptism, forever changed. It is a journey marked by the enduring truth of Philippians 1:6, "And I am sure of this, that he who began a good work in you will bring it to completion at the day of Jesus Christ." Baptism marks the beginning of a work of transformation that continues throughout a believer's life—a journey from glory to glory.

In conclusion, baptism is not a mere ritual but a gateway to personal transformation—a journey where the old self is left behind, and the new self emerges. It inspires positive changes in lives, relationships, and actions, echoing the transformative power of God's grace. As believers, we continue to grow and be sanctified, knowing that the impact of baptism endures, shaping us into the likeness of Christ, and leading us on a path of personal transformation that reflects the glory of our Savior.

Caleb's Renewal: The Healing
Waters of Baptism

Caleb, a seasoned police officer in a bustling city, had seen his share of life's darker moments. The challenges of his profession left him with a heart weighed down by cynicism and a lingering anger that colored his relationships and clouded his judgment. His life, though successful on the surface, was marred by internal struggles that he kept hidden behind a facade of toughness.

One rainy afternoon, driven by a sense of desperate need for change, Caleb attended a community church service, where he was moved by the pastor's sermon on the transformative power of baptism, quoting 2 Corinthians 5:17, "Therefore, if anyone is in Christ, he is a new creation. The old has passed away; behold, the new has come." The message struck a chord in Caleb, awakening a yearning for a fresh start and a new identity in Christ.

After weeks of contemplation and attending baptism classes, Caleb decided to take the plunge—literally and figuratively. His baptism was not just a ceremonial immersion; it was an earnest plea for renewal and a heartfelt surrender to a greater power capable of transforming his life.

Emerging from the baptismal waters, Caleb felt as if a heavy burden had been lifted from his shoulders. He experienced an overwhelming sense of peace and a newness of spirit that he had not felt in years. The act of baptism marked the beginning of his journey from a life of bitterness to one of forgiveness, from despair to hope.

Inspired by his new faith, Caleb began to mend his strained relationships. He reached out to old friends he had wronged and sought forgiveness from family members he had alienated. Each step towards reconciliation was a testament to the personal transformation initiated by his baptism.

The changes in Caleb were not only emotional and relational but also practical. He started volunteering at a local youth center, mentoring young people and sharing his story of transformation. His testimony of change was powerful and authentic, resonating with many who were struggling with their own issues of anger and resentment.

Moreover, Caleb's approach to his police work transformed. He became more compassionate and patient in his interactions, embodying the principles of kindness and forgiveness that he learned from Ephesians 4:31–32. His colleagues noticed the change, often seeking his advice when dealing with difficult situations.

Caleb's story of baptism and personal transformation became a beacon of hope within his community and church. His journey from a hardened police officer to a compassionate community leader was a powerful illustration of baptism's profound impact on a person's life.

In conclusion, Caleb's story exemplifies how baptism is much more than a symbolic act—it is a gateway to profound personal transformation. It marks the beginning of a new existence where the old self is left behind, and a new self, shaped by grace and forged in the waters of renewal, begins to emerge. Caleb continues to walk this path of transformation, each step a reflection of the continuing work of God in his life, as promised in Philippians 1:6, inspiring others to seek their own stories of renewal and change.

Conclusion

As we conclude our exploration of Chapter 8, "Integrating the Rite: Baptism's Place in the Believer's Walk," we find ourselves at a crossroads of profound significance. Our journey through these pages has revealed that baptism is not a stagnant moment but a dynamic force—an ever-flowing river of grace that shapes our character, values, and spiritual disciplines.

We've journeyed alongside individuals who have tasted the waters of baptism and found them to be not just life-giving but life-transforming. Their stories bear witness to the enduring power of baptism, its capacity to mend the broken, heal the wounded, and inspire hope where there was despair. We've witnessed personal transformation, from brokenness to wholeness, from bitterness to forgiveness, from despair to hope, echoing the Apostle Paul's words in 2 Corinthians 5:17: "Therefore, if anyone is in Christ, he is a new creation. The old has passed away; behold, the new has come."

Baptism is more than a ceremony; it is an encounter—an encounter with the living God that sets in motion a lifelong journey of becoming. It shapes our character, values, and daily practices, calling us to live out the truth of Philippians 2:13: "For it is God who works in you, both to will and to work for his good pleasure." Our spiritual formation is not a solitary endeavor but a partnership with the Divine Potter, who molds us into vessels of grace.

As we conclude this chapter, may we carry with us the profound truth that baptism is not just a memory but a mission. It calls us to daily immersion in the waters of God's Word, prayer, and acts of love and service. It beckons us to live out our identity as children of God, to press on toward the upward call, and to become more like the One in whose name we were baptized.

The journey continues beyond these pages—a journey of ongoing transformation, where the waters of baptism flow into every corner of our lives, shaping us into vessels of grace, purpose, and unwavering faith. As we step into the chapters ahead, may we do so with hearts open to the ongoing work of transformation, knowing that the enduring impact of baptism continues to shape us into the image of Christ, and the journey is far from over.

CHAPTER NINE

The Ripple Effect: Community and Baptismal Experience

"Just as a body, though one, has many parts, but all its many parts form one body, so it is with Christ. For we were all baptized by one Spirit so as to form one body—whether Jews or Gentiles, slave or free—and we were all given the one Spirit to drink."
—1 CORINTHIANS 12:12–13 NIV

In the vast expanse of human experience, there are moments that transcend the ordinary, moments that touch the very core of our existence, and moments that resonate through time and eternity. Baptism, the transformative act of being drenched in faith, is one such profound moment. Yet, the impact of baptism extends far beyond the individual taking the plunge. It creates ripples, like pebbles cast into a serene pond, that reverberate through the lives of believers and the faith community at large. In Chapter 9, "The Ripple Effect: Community and Baptismal Experience," we embark on a journey to explore the intricate interplay between baptism and the faith community.

This is a chapter that delves into the communal heart of faith, where the role of the faith community is not merely that of a bystander but of an active participant, an encourager, and a mentor. It is a chapter that celebrates the richness of baptismal traditions and the shared tapestry of faith that unites believers from various denominations. In these pages, we discover that baptism is not just a solitary experience but a communal celebration, and its ripples extend far beyond the waters of the baptismal font, shaping lives and hearts within the faith community.

Within the intricate tapestry of human existence, there emerge moments that transcend the ordinary, touching the very core of our being. Baptism, the transformative act of being drenched in faith, stands as one such profound moment. Yet, the influence of baptism extends far beyond the individual who steps into the waters of faith. It sets in motion ripples, akin to pebbles cast into the still surface of a serene pond, which reverberate through the lives of believers and resonate within the faith community at large.

The Role of the Faith Community

In the tapestry of our faith journeys, there exists a thread so intricate, so vital, that it weaves through every moment of our spiritual transformation—the faith community. When it comes to the transformative act of water baptism, this community becomes not merely a backdrop but an essential catalyst for a profound and lasting experience.

Scripture tells us in Hebrews 10:24–25, "And let us consider how to stir up one another to love and good works, not neglecting to meet together, as is the habit of some, but encouraging one another, and all the more as you see the Day drawing near." In the context of baptism, this encouragement takes on a special significance. The faith community becomes a source of support, mentorship, and encouragement for those preparing to take the plunge, guiding them through the waters of faith.

Baptism is not a solitary act but a communal celebration— a declaration that resonates beyond the individual and into the hearts of believers gathered. Just as the body is made up of many parts, the faith community is a diverse tapestry of individuals, each playing a unique role in the baptismal journey. In 1 Corinthians 12:26, we read, "If one member suffers, all suffer together; if one member is honored, all rejoice together." This truth is profoundly realized in the communal celebration of baptism, where the joy of one becomes the joy of all, and the transformation of one becomes a testament to the power of faith shared.

Mentors within the faith community take on a sacred role, much like seasoned guides on a treacherous mountain ascent. They offer wisdom, guidance, and companionship to those journeying toward baptism, echoing the words of Galatians 6:2, "Bear one another's burdens, and so fulfill the law of Christ." Through mentorship, candidates are not alone in their preparations; they are embraced by a community that carries their burdens, celebrates their victories, and walks alongside them in faith.

In conclusion, the faith community is not a mere backdrop but an active participant in the baptismal journey. It embodies the biblical call to encourage, support, and bear one another's burdens. Through the shared celebration of baptism and the guidance of mentors, the faith community transforms a solitary act into a communal commitment—a beautiful ripple effect of faith that extends far beyond the waters of baptism, shaping lives and hearts in the process.

Woven Waters: The Community's Role in the Baptismal Journey

In a quaint town nestled between rolling hills and bustling streams, there lived a young woman named Julia. Julia, though curious and spirited, had long felt a void within her, an emptiness that echoed through her mundane routines. Her encounter with the local faith community led her to consider baptism—a step she hoped would fill the void and offer a new direction in her life.

As Julia approached her baptism, the role of the faith community became profoundly evident. Each member, from elderly Mrs. Jackson to young pastor Mike, played a vital part in preparing her for this spiritual milestone. They shared scriptures, stories of their own faith journeys, and spent many evenings in prayer with her, creating a mosaic of support that was both uplifting and transformative.

Mrs. Jackson, who had seen many come to the waters of baptism, took it upon herself to mentor Julia. She was like a skilled gardener, knowing when to offer water, when to prune, and when to simply watch and let the sun do its work. She shared with Julia the powerful words of Hebrews 10:24–25, reminding her of the importance of community and mutual encouragement.

The day of Julia's baptism arrived, a clear, crisp morning, as if the very weather itself was in celebration. The church was filled with faces, some familiar and some new, all united in their support for her. As Julia stepped into the baptismal pool, the water cool against her skin, she felt the weight of her past and her uncertainties dissolve into a profound peace.

As she rose from the water, the congregation erupted in joyous applause, a physical manifestation of 1 Corinthians 12:26, where each member shares in the joy and transformation of one another. The shared joy was palpable, enveloping Julia in a warmth that far exceeded the physical embrace of the water.

Post-baptism, Julia found her relationship with the community deepening. Guided by the steadfast mentorship of Mrs. Jackson and supported by the collective strength of the community, she navigated the new challenges of her faith journey. Each hurdle, each moment of doubt, was met not with judgment but with encouragement and wisdom, particularly reflecting Galatians 6:2, where the community bore one another's burdens, fulfilling the law of Christ.

Julia's story is a testament to the vital role of the faith community in the baptismal experience. It wasn't just about the act of being baptized but about being woven into a tapestry of believers, each thread strengthening the other, each story adding depth and color to her own. This transformative journey marked not just a renewal of spirit but a profound integration into a body that echoed through eternity, a ripple effect of faith that transformed not only her life but also enriched the collective soul of the community.

Baptismal Preparation and Mentoring

In the tapestry of faith, preparation and guidance are the threads that intricately weave together the beautiful mosaic of baptism. Properly preparing individuals for this transformative experience and providing them with seasoned mentors is akin to offering a sturdy vessel for a journey across turbulent waters. It is a sacred duty that the faith community embraces with unwavering commitment.

The wisdom of Proverbs 15:22 reminds us that "Without counsel plans fail, but with many advisers, they succeed." In the context of baptism, this counsel is a beacon of hope, a guiding light for those embarking on a spiritual voyage. The journey toward baptism involves more than just a leap into water; it is a profound act of faith and commitment. Churches and faith communities, like loving captains, should equip candidates with the knowledge and understanding necessary for this journey.

Mentors, often seasoned believers who have traversed these waters before, play an invaluable role in this preparation. They become guides, confidants, and encouragers, embodying the spirit of Galatians 6:2: "Bear one another's burdens, and so fulfill the law of Christ." Through mentorship, candidates are not left to navigate the waters of faith alone. They are embraced by a community that carries their burdens, celebrates their victories, and walks alongside them in faith.

Consider the story of Erica, a young woman preparing for baptism. She found herself grappling with doubts and uncertainties as the day approached. But with a mentor by her side, someone who had journeyed through similar waters, Erica found the reassurance and guidance she needed. Together, they explored the depths of faith, studied Scripture, and prayed fervently.

Erica's mentor shared their own baptismal journey, revealing the profound impact it had on their life. In this exchange, not only did Erica find strength, but her mentor found renewed purpose in witnessing the transformative power of faith through the eyes of a candidate.

Stories like Erica's echo the truth of Ecclesiastes 4:9–10: "Two are better than one because they have a good reward for their toil. For if they fall, one will lift up his fellow." The preparation and mentorship process is a powerful reminder that in the body of Christ, we are not solitary travelers but companions on the same journey, lifting each other up in faith.

In conclusion, baptismal preparation and mentoring are the building blocks of a profound and transformative baptismal experience. Through guidance, education, and support, churches and faith communities equip candidates to take the plunge of faith. And through the loving presence of mentors, candidates find strength and assurance, while mentors themselves witness the enduring impact of baptism through the eyes of those they guide. It is a journey marked by the beauty of shared faith, preparation, and transformation— a ripple effect that extends throughout the faith community.

Shared Waters: The Journey of Mentorship and Transformation in Baptismal Preparation

In the small coastal town of Seaview, the local church stood as a beacon of guidance and unity, its spire reaching towards the heavens as if to physically manifest its spiritual aspirations. At the heart of this community was the Baptism Preparation Program, a finely woven tapestry of mentorship and preparation that not only readied individuals for baptism but profoundly deepened the communal bonds.

Cain, a 30-year-old carpenter, found himself drawn to the waters of baptism, seeking a renewal not only of faith but of purpose. Despite his robust exterior, Cain carried the weight of past failures and sought redemption and a fresh start. He was introduced to Daniel, a seasoned mentor in the community, known for his gentle spirit and wise counsel. Daniel had navigated many storms, both at sea and in spirit, and his journey resonated deeply with Cain.

Together, they embarked on a journey of preparation that was as much about building a vessel of faith as it was about mending the cracks in Cain's weary heart. They met weekly, discussing scriptures and life challenges, where Proverbs 15:22 often guided their sessions: "Without counsel plans fail, but with many advisers, they succeed." Daniel's role transcended that of a guide; he became a confidant and a mirror reflecting the potential he saw in Cain.

As the day of the baptism approached, the ripples of Cain's transformation were already palpable. His interactions within the community shifted from distant to engaged. He volunteered where help was needed, embodying the spirit of Galatians 6:2, "Bear one another's burdens, and so fulfill the law of Christ." The change in Cain stirred a renewed vigor in

Daniel too, who saw in Cain the echoes of his own transformative journey.

The baptism itself was a communal celebration, where the faith community came together not just as witnesses but as active participants in the sacred act. As Cain emerged from the baptismal waters, the congregation erupted in joyous applause, not merely for the act itself but for the journey it represented— a journey of mutual upliftment and communal strength.

Lacy, another member of the community and a recent convert, watched with tear-filled eyes. Inspired by Cain's journey and the palpable bond he shared with Daniel, she approached the mentorship program, ready to weave her thread into the tapestry of their shared faith. Her decision was a testament to the ripple effect of Cain's transformation, illustrating how one life uplifted in faith could resonate through the hearts of many.

The story of Cain and Daniel, their challenges and triumphs, became a cornerstone of the Baptism Preparation Program. It served as a profound reminder that baptism was not a conclusion but a commencement—a perpetual journey of faith not walked alone but alongside a community, each step marked by shared burdens and multiplied joys.

Baptismal Celebrations and Traditions

In the diverse tapestry of Christianity, baptismal celebrations and traditions are like colorful threads, each unique yet woven together in the grand design of faith. These practices, observed by various Christian denominations and faith communities, are not mere rituals but profound expressions of faith that enrich the baptismal journey.

1 Corinthians 12:12–13 reminds us, "For just as the body is one and has many members, and all the members of the body, though many, are one body, so it is with Christ. For in one Spirit, we were all baptized into one body—Jews or Greeks, slaves or free—and all were made to drink of one Spirit." These words reflect the unity of the faith community, transcending differences in tradition and practice. It is this unity that baptismal celebrations and traditions aim to affirm.

Take, for example, the beautiful tradition of the white baptismal gown, often seen in many denominations. It symbolizes purity and newness of life, echoing the words of Revelation 7:14: "They have washed their robes and made them white in the blood of the Lamb." When candidates don this garment, they are reminded of their identity as cleansed and transformed followers of Christ. This simple act binds them not only to the community they are joining but to the centuries-old tradition of Christian faith.

In other traditions, such as the anointing with oil or the use of water from the Jordan River, symbolism is rich and profound. These practices connect candidates to the historical and biblical roots of their faith, reminding them that their journey is part of a larger narrative. In Romans 6:4, we read, "We were buried therefore with him by baptism into death, in order that, just as Christ was raised from the dead by the glory of the Father, we too might walk in newness of life." These traditions amplify the significance of the moment, inviting candidates to step into the waters of faith with a profound sense of belonging and identity.

Beyond symbolism, baptismal celebrations and traditions foster a sense of community and shared faith. They create a collective memory, a legacy that bridges generations of believers. When a congregation gathers to witness a baptism, they are not mere spectators but active participants in a sacred moment.

In conclusion, baptismal celebrations and traditions are a testament to the richness and diversity of Christian faith. They unite believers across denominations, reminding us that, regardless of our differences, we share a common identity in Christ. These practices bring depth and significance to the baptismal experience, grounding candidates in their faith and fostering a profound sense of belonging within the faith community. As we explore these traditions, we discover that, like a symphony of many instruments playing in harmony, they contribute to the beautiful melody of our shared faith—a melody that resounds through the ages.

United in Waters: Celebrating Diversity and Unity in Baptismal Traditions

In the quaint village of Stonewater, a tapestry of diverse Christian traditions weaves the community tightly together, each thread vibrant with its unique color yet harmoniously blending into a beautiful whole. At the heart of this unity is the local church, a beacon of togetherness, where every year, the community celebrates its rich variety of baptismal practices in a unique gathering known as the "Festival of Baptisms."

The festival is a day marked by joy, reverence, and an educational journey through the world of Christian traditions. At the center of the village green, stands a large, open-sided tent, adorned with symbols from various denominations—crosses, icons, oils, and waters from rivers as sacred as the Jordan.

Among the attendees is Luna, a young teacher new to the village, who was deeply moved by the collective spirit of the event. Luna had always felt a disconnect between her personal faith journey and the broader Christian community due to her mixed-denominational background. However, the festival provided a transformative understanding of how traditions could vary yet share a profound common purpose.

As Luna wandered from one exhibit to another, she was drawn to the station displaying white baptismal gowns, each embroidered with intricate patterns symbolizing purity and renewal. Here, she learned that these gowns represented a shared identity in Christ, as echoed in Revelation 7:14, about believers washing their robes white in the blood of the Lamb. This visual and tangible connection to the faith of generations past touched Luna profoundly, embedding a sense of belonging.

Another station featured the anointing with oil, where she watched as believers were anointed, a practice symbolizing the Holy Spirit's consecration of the believer for God's service. This ritual, reminiscent of ancient customs, illustrated the continuity and depth of their faith's historical and biblical roots, as described in Romans 6:4 about being buried and raised with Christ.

The highlight for Luna was the communal baptism ceremony, a vibrant, collective affirmation of faith where participants from different backgrounds were baptized together in a large pool. This act was not just about individual declarations of faith but a powerful symbol of unity—diverse yet united in Christ as described in 1 Corinthians 12:12–13.

Moved by this experience, Luna decided to write about the festival for the local newsletter, emphasizing how the rich tapestry of traditions at the festival not only honored individual journeys but also strengthened the communal bonds of faith. Her article celebrated the profound impact of these traditions in fostering a sense of belonging and identity among believers, reinforcing that while the expressions of faith might vary, the essence of baptism as a transformative journey in Christ remains constant.

The story of the Festival of Baptisms in Stonewater reminds us of the beautiful interplay between tradition and transformation within the Christian faith, a harmony that resonates deeply within the community and enriches every believer's journey.

―――――

Conclusion

As we draw the curtain on Chapter 9, we find ourselves standing on the shores of a profound truth—a truth that resounds through the ages: Baptism, the transformative act of faith, is not a solitary endeavor but a communal celebration. In the mosaic of human existence, it is the faith community that shapes the baptismal journey, adding depth, meaning, and unity to the experience.

We have journeyed through the pages of this chapter, witnessing how the faith community, in obedience to the biblical call, becomes the scaffold upon which candidates for baptism are supported, prepared, and mentored. It is a community that embodies Galatians 6:2, "Bear one another's burdens, and so fulfill the law of Christ," ensuring that the journey toward baptism is not a solitary trek but a shared expedition.

We have met mentors who, like seasoned guides on a mountain ascent, walk alongside candidates, offering wisdom, encouragement, and companionship. Through their stories, we have glimpsed the enduring impact of baptism through the eyes of those who guide and those who are guided.

We have explored the rich tapestry of baptismal traditions, each thread representing a unique expression of faith and identity within the diverse body of Christ. These traditions have provided a profound sense of belonging, connecting candidates to the historical and biblical roots of their faith.

In conclusion, we are reminded that the act of baptism is not confined to the moment one steps into the waters—it is a journey that continues long after the droplets have dried. Baptismal ripples echo through the lives of believers, weaving a communal tapestry of faith that transcends denominational boundaries. As we close this chapter, we carry with us the understanding that, in the grand symphony of faith, each note plays a vital role, and every ripple created by the faith community extends the melody of shared faith, preparation, and transformation, a melody that resounds through the ages.

CHAPTER TEN

Streams of Controversy: Addressing Common Questions and Challenges

"Peter replied, 'Repent and be baptized, every one of you, in the name of Jesus Christ for the forgiveness of your sins. And you will receive the gift of the Holy Spirit.'" —ACTS 2:38 NIV

As we stand on the banks of the river of faith, gazing at the sacred waters of baptism, we are reminded that this timeless sacrament flows through the pages of Christian history like a steadfast river. Its significance is profound, its symbolism rich, and its impact transformative. Yet, in the vast riverbed of theological discourse and within the complex delta of human experience, the waters of baptism encounter a myriad of tributaries—debates, questions, and cultural shifts-that shape its course and character.

These tributaries are not to be feared or dismissed but to be explored, for they offer us the opportunity to delve deeper into the meaning and purpose of this ancient rite. In this final chapter of our journey, we embark on an exploration of these theological currents and cultural undercurrents. We will wade into the depths of debates, clarify common questions, and navigate the complex challenges that often surround the transformative act of water baptism.

Our mission is to seek clarity, understanding, and biblical insight, providing you, dear reader, with a map to navigate the complexities and controversies that sometimes muddy the waters of baptism. As we journey together, remember that beneath the surface turbulence, the waters of baptism remain a wellspring of faith, grace, and transformation. These waters flow not only through the annals of history but through the depths of the human soul.

Join us as we chart the course through these streams of controversy, always mindful of the enduring and transformative power of baptism in the life of the believer and the life of the Church.

Theological Debates Surrounding Baptism

In the flowing currents of Christianity's rich history, the subject of baptism has often been a source of theological debate, shaping the faith and practice of believers throughout the ages. Like a river with its tributaries, these debates have given rise to various streams of thought. One such stream centers around the notion of baptismal regeneration, where the act of baptism is seen as a means of receiving God's grace and salvation.

Titus 3:5 reminds us, "He saved us, not because of righteous things we had done, but because of his mercy. He saved us through the washing of rebirth and renewal by the Holy Spirit." This verse reflects the belief that baptism marks the beginning of a new life in Christ, infused with His grace. However, this perspective flows alongside other theological currents that emphasize faith as the sole requirement for salvation, raising questions about the role of baptism in the process.

These debates also extend to the age at which baptism is administered, with some advocating for infant baptism as a covenantal sign, while others assert that only believers who can make a conscious confession of faith should be baptized. Moreover, discussions about the mode of baptism—whether by immersion, pouring, or sprinkling—continue to stir theological waters. The diversity of views on these topics underscores the complexity of baptism's theological landscape, a terrain where believers and theologians alike tread in search of deeper understanding and unity.

As we navigate these theological debates, it is essential to recognize the rich tapestry of thought that has emerged from

Christian history. Despite differences in interpretation, the central focus remains the transformative power of baptism as a sacred and spiritually significant act. In the midst of these currents of thought, Christians are united by their recognition of baptism's profound impact on the believer's journey of faith, an impact that transcends theological divides and flows toward a shared commitment to follow Christ.

As we explore these theological debates, we must also acknowledge the importance of dialogue and respect for differing perspectives within the Christian community. Romans 14:1 encourages believers to "accept the one whose faith is weak, without quarreling over disputable matters." In the spirit of unity and love, Christians have engaged in respectful discourse throughout history, seeking to understand the diverse theological viewpoints surrounding baptism.

One of the streams in this theological river is the belief in baptismal regeneration, which finds its roots in passages like Acts 2:38, where Peter exhorts the crowd to "repent and be baptized, every one of you, in the name of Jesus Christ for the forgiveness of your sins." This perspective sees baptism as a means through which God imparts His grace and forgives sins. However, others argue that salvation is solely by grace through faith, as emphasized in Ephesians 2:8–9, where it is written, "For it is by grace you have been saved, through faith—and this is not from yourselves, it is the gift of God." These contrasting viewpoints continue to be points of theological reflection and discussion.

Another branch of this theological river pertains to the age at which baptism should be administered. Proponents of infant baptism draw from the biblical tradition of circumcision, considering it a parallel to the New Testament practice of baptizing infants as a sign of God's covenant.

Conversely, believers' baptism asserts that baptism should follow a conscious confession of faith, exemplified by passages like Acts 8:12, where "they believed Philip as he proclaimed the good news of the kingdom of God and the name of Jesus Christ; they were baptized, both men and women." This debate, too, underscores the diversity of perspectives within the Christian tradition.

Finally, the mode of baptism, whether by immersion, pouring, or sprinkling, has been a point of contention and reflection. Some argue for immersion, symbolizing the death, burial, and resurrection of Christ, as depicted in Romans 6:3–4. Others find merit in the symbolism of pouring or sprinkling, mirroring the outpouring of the Holy Spirit, as in Acts 2:17. These different modes reflect the richness of Christian tradition and interpretation.

In conclusion, the theological debates surrounding baptism are not merely historical artifacts but ongoing conversations within the Christian community. They serve as reminders that faith is a dynamic journey, marked by sincere efforts to understand and live out the teachings of Christ. While differing theological currents may exist, they flow toward a shared commitment to the transformative power of baptism as a sacred and spiritually significant act, uniting believers in their devotion to Christ and His message of redemption and renewal.

Navigating the Waters of Faith: The Story of Pastor Simon and the Baptism Debates

Pastor Simon stood at the river's edge, watching the gentle flow of the water, reflecting on the heated discussions that had recently taken place in his congregation. The debates about baptism's role in salvation, its appropriate age, and the correct mode had stirred the waters of his community, much like the river before him.

Simon had always cherished baptism's sacred tradition, seeing it as a profound declaration of faith and a critical moment in a believer's spiritual journey. Yet, he faced a congregation divided by differing theological perspectives. Some members insisted on baptism by immersion only, citing it as the truest representation of Christ's death and resurrection. Others argued for the inclusion of infant baptism, seeing it as a continuation of the covenant promises evident in Scripture.

The contention had reached a peak during a congregational meeting where arguments echoed around the room, each member clinging tightly to their doctrinal positions. It was then that Pastor Simon decided to embark on a journey—a journey to weave through these theological debates with grace and understanding, guiding his congregation toward unity.

Drawing from the scripture, Titus 3:5, which highlighted baptism as a renewal by the Holy Spirit, Simon organized a series of study sessions. He invited theologians from different denominations to speak, offering insights into the diverse practices of baptism within the global church. These sessions were designed not to debate but to deepen understanding and respect for varied practices.

One poignant session involved a discussion on Acts 2:38. Simon used this to show how baptism served as a response to God's grace, a public testament to personal faith. He shared stories from church history, illustrating how early Christians navigated their own baptismal debates. Through these stories, he emphasized the common thread—the transformative power of baptism, regardless of the method or timing.

The series reached its climax with a shared baptism service. Members who had argued against each other weeks before now stood side by side at the river's edge. There, they witnessed several baptisms: immersion for some, pouring for others. Simon had arranged for individuals from different backgrounds to share their testimonies, each story a testament to the personal and communal transformation baptism had ignited in their lives.

As the congregation listened, something remarkable happened. The rigid lines of theological debate softened. Understanding blossomed. A young man, initially skeptical of infant baptism, found himself moved by a story of a family dedicating their child to God through baptism, vowing to raise him in the faith until he could claim it as his own.

The service concluded with the congregation singing hymns by the water, their voices blending into a harmonious expression of shared faith. Pastor Simon looked around, his heart full, as he saw the joy and unity in his congregation's eyes. They had come together not by resolving all their theological differences but by recognizing the deeper bond they shared in Christ.

In that moment, the river seemed to mirror the congregation—a confluence of different streams, each distinct, yet part of a greater whole. Pastor Simon knew the debates wouldn't disappear, but he was confident that his congregation now had the tools and the heart to engage them with love and respect. They had learned that the waters of baptism were indeed deep and wide, capable of holding all their beliefs in one embrace.

From that day forward, the story of their riverside reconciliation became a cornerstone of their community, a reminder of how faith could bridge differences and how baptism, in all its forms, remained a powerful testament to life in Christ.

———————

Common Questions and Misconceptions

In the meandering river of Christian beliefs and practices, questions and misconceptions often swirl like eddies. It is crucial to address these inquiries and clarify misunderstandings, providing the firm ground of biblical truth for those navigating the waters of baptism. One common question that arises is the necessity of baptism for salvation. Some wonder if baptism is a prerequisite for receiving God's grace.

In response, it is essential to turn to the clear waters of Scripture. Acts 2:38 tells us, "Repent and be baptized, every one of you, in the name of Jesus Christ for the forgiveness of your sins." Here, baptism is closely linked with repentance and the forgiveness of sins, but it is faith in Christ that opens the door to salvation. As Ephesians 2:8–9 reminds us, "For it is by grace you have been saved, through faith—and this is not from yourselves, it is the gift of God." Baptism, then, is a response to God's grace and an outward declaration of faith, a step of obedience in the journey of salvation.

Another question that often surfaces concerns the age of baptismal candidates. Is baptism reserved for adults who can make a conscious decision of faith, or can infants be baptized? The answer lies in a nuanced understanding of Scripture. While the New Testament portrays adults making a conscious confession of faith and being baptized, it also underscores the significance of God's covenant with families.

Acts 16:15 recounts the baptism of Lydia's household, indicating that entire families, including children, were included in this covenant act. Baptism, in this context, serves as a sign of God's grace extended to the believing community, including children. However, it is essential to recognize that as children mature, they are encouraged to make their faith their own through personal confession and ongoing discipleship.

Repentance is another pivotal element in baptismal theology. Some may wonder about the role of repentance in the act of baptism. Acts 3:19 provides insight, urging, "Repent, then, and turn to God, so that your sins may be wiped out, that times of refreshing may come from the Lord." Repentance is like the riverbanks that guide and contain the flow of baptism. It is a turning away from sin and a turning toward God, paving the way for the cleansing waters of baptism to symbolize forgiveness and newness of life. Baptism and repentance are intertwined, marking a profound moment of transformation.

In addressing these common questions and misconceptions, we find that the waters of baptism flow in harmony with the clear currents of Scripture. They offer a profound opportunity to express faith, receive God's grace, and experience the transformative power of repentance.

Baptism is a journey of obedience, a declaration of faith, and a response to God's covenant love—a sacred act that invites believers to wade deeper into the waters of His grace and truth.

Bridging Beliefs: The Story of Pastor Isabel and the Baptism Workshop

Pastor Isabel stood before her diverse congregation, a community marked by a rich tapestry of backgrounds and beliefs about baptism. She knew the importance of addressing the swirling eddies of confusion and contention that sometimes clouded their understanding of this sacred act. Determined to offer clarity and foster unity, Pastor Isabel decided to organize a workshop titled "Wading Through the Waters: Understanding Baptism."

The day of the workshop, the church hall buzzed with anticipation. Isabel began with a prayer for openness and understanding, then dived into the common questions and misconceptions surrounding baptism. She started with the necessity of baptism for salvation, a topic that often sparked heated debates.

Using Acts 2:38 and Ephesians 2:8–9, she explained the relationship between baptism, repentance, and faith. "Baptism," she stated, "is closely linked with repentance and the forgiveness of sins, but it is through faith that we receive salvation. Baptism is our outward response to God's inward grace."

Next, she addressed the question of the age at which baptism should be administered. She discussed the practice of infant baptism and believers' baptism, sharing Acts

16:15 where Caroline's entire household was baptized. "Baptism extends God's grace to families, symbolizing inclusion in the faith community. Yet, as our children grow, we encourage them to embrace and affirm their faith personally," Isabel explained.

She then turned to the role of repentance, highlighted by Acts 3:19, describing it as essential in preparing one's heart for baptism. "Repentance and baptism are intertwined," she taught, "each reinforcing the profound transformation we undergo as followers of Christ."

Throughout the workshop, Isabel facilitated discussions where members shared their experiences and insights, enriching everyone's understanding. Among the attendees was Collin, a new member who had struggled with the idea of baptizing his infant daughter. The discussions helped him appreciate the covenantal aspect of baptism, seeing it as a starting point of faith that his daughter would grow into.

As the workshop concluded, Isabel invited the participants to gather around a small pool set up at the front of the hall. Here, they conducted a reaffirmation of baptism ceremony. One by one, members dipped their hands in the water, each praying a commitment to live out their baptism in faith and obedience.

The event was transformative. Not only did it clear up misconceptions, but it also united the congregation in a deeper understanding of their shared faith. Collin, moved by the experience, decided to have his daughter baptized the following month, inviting the whole congregation to witness and support his family's faith journey.

Isabel's initiative had turned a potential division into a deepening of faith, illustrating how addressing common questions and misconceptions with biblical truth can guide a community to greater unity and commitment. As members left the hall that day, they felt more connected not only to their faith but to each other, ready to support one another in their spiritual journeys.

In Pastor Isabel's church, baptism became more than a ritual; it was a shared journey of faith, marked by a collective commitment to live out the transformative power of God's grace and truth.

Contemporary Challenges and Cultural Context

In the ever-flowing river of Christian tradition, the practice and understanding of baptism are not immune to the currents of contemporary challenges and shifting cultural landscapes. As we navigate these waters, we encounter the strong undercurrent of secularism—a worldview that often dismisses or marginalizes matters of faith. In this context, the practice of baptism may be met with skepticism or indifference.

Yet, we are reminded of Matthew 28:19–20, where Jesus commissioned His disciples to "go and make disciples of all nations, baptizing them in the name of the Father and of the

Son and of the Holy Spirit, and teaching them to obey everything I have commanded you." These words remain a beacon of hope, urging believers to continue baptizing and teaching, even in the face of secular challenges. Baptism, in this context, becomes a powerful counter-narrative, a visible declaration of one's commitment to Christ in a world that often values materialism and self-indulgence.

Another current shaping contemporary perspectives on baptism is religious pluralism. In today's interconnected world, people of various faiths and beliefs coexist, and this pluralistic landscape can influence how individuals perceive the significance of baptism. It prompts questions about exclusivity versus inclusivity, about whether baptism is a symbol of one's personal faith journey or an assertion of a particular religious tradition. Here, 1 Corinthians 12:13 offers guidance: "For we were all baptized by one Spirit so as to form one body—whether Jews or Gentiles, slave or free—and we were all given the one Spirit to drink." Baptism, seen through the lens of unity, underscores the idea that believers from diverse backgrounds are brought into the one body of Christ through the work of the Holy Spirit. It transcends religious divisions, inviting all into a deeper relationship with God.

Moreover, we encounter shifting views on spirituality within contemporary society. The waters of spirituality are vast and varied, with many individuals seeking meaning and connection outside traditional religious structures. In such a context, baptism may be viewed as one spiritual practice among many, leading to questions about its uniqueness and necessity. Here, we turn to Colossians 2:12, which speaks of baptism as an act of faith "in the working of God, who raised Him [Christ] from the dead." Baptism, as a sacrament rooted in the resurrection of Christ, carries a unique spiritual significance. It invites individuals to participate in the divine drama of death and resurrection, offering a profound encounter with the living God.

In response to these contemporary challenges and cultural shifts, churches can adapt by emphasizing the transformative and communal aspects of baptism. Baptism is not merely a ritual but a journey of faith and a communal celebration of God's grace. By fostering an environment of inclusivity, understanding, and spiritual depth, churches can respond effectively to the changing world, ensuring that the waters of baptism continue to flow as a source of spiritual renewal and transformation for all seekers of truth and meaning.

Navigating New Waters: Rev. Bartholomew's Community Baptism Initiative

In the heart of a bustling city marked by a mosaic of cultures and beliefs, Rev. Bartholomew faced the challenge of bringing the ancient practice of baptism into a modern, pluralistic society. His church, a small but vibrant congregation, sat at the intersection of several different neighborhoods, each home to people of varied religious and cultural backgrounds. Rev. Bartholomew recognized the need to address the contemporary challenges that influenced perceptions of baptism and its role in the community.

Inspired by the teachings of Matthew 28:19–20, Rev. Bartholomew launched the "Baptism Without Borders" initiative. His goal was to present baptism not just as a ritual of individual faith, but as a celebration of community and spiritual renewal that transcended cultural and religious boundaries.

To kick off the initiative, Rev. Bartholomew organized a series of community forums. These forums served as open spaces for dialogue about spiritual beliefs, the significance of baptism in different traditions, and the role of faith in contemporary society. He invited leaders from various faith communities to share their perspectives, fostering a spirit of inclusivity and mutual respect. The forums highlighted baptism's unique place in Christian tradition while acknowledging the rich spiritual practices of other faiths.

Rev. Bartholomew also addressed the skepticism and indifference that often met religious practices in a secular world. He emphasized baptism's transformative power, as described in Colossians 2:12, discussing how it symbolized a personal and communal rebirth and resurrection. He presented baptism as a pathway not only to personal transformation but as a commitment to community service and social justice, resonating with secular values of self-improvement and community betterment.

The highlight of the initiative was a public baptism event held at a local park. It was designed as a community celebration, complete with music, food, and storytelling. Those who chose to be baptized were invited to share their stories of faith, doubt, and hope. This event not only celebrated the baptisms but also the collective journey of the community towards understanding and spiritual depth.

As individuals from various backgrounds stepped into the baptismal waters, it became a powerful counter-narrative to the prevailing secularism and religious pluralism. Each baptism was a visible declaration of faith, yet it was also a statement of unity and diversity, echoing 1 Corinthians 12:13's message of unity in diversity through the Holy Spirit.

The "Baptism Without Borders" initiative gradually transformed the community's perception of baptism. It became viewed as a meaningful spiritual practice that was inclusive and relevant. Local media covered the event, further extending its impact and fostering broader conversations about the role of faith in modern society.

In response to the shifting views on spirituality, Rev. Bartholomew ensured that the church remained a place of openness and dialogue. The church's doors were always open, inviting all who sought spiritual connection and community engagement, regardless of their faith background.

Rev. Bartholomew's initiative not only revitalized the practice of baptism within his church but also strengthened the bonds within the community. It showed that, even in a world of diverse and often conflicting beliefs, shared spiritual experiences could foster unity and collective growth. The waters of baptism, flowing through this urban landscape, became a source of renewal and hope, nurturing a community bonded by its commitment to spiritual exploration and mutual respect.

———————

Conclusion

As we bring our journey through the swirling currents of baptismal theology and practice to a close, we find ourselves standing on the riverbank, gazing back at the winding path we've traveled. The waters of baptism have carried us through deep theological debates, answered common questions, and navigated the complex challenges of our ever-changing world.

In these streams of controversy, we've discovered that, like any river, baptism flows through history with both clarity and mystery. It is a sacred act that unites believers across time and culture, binding them together in the shared experience of faith and transformation. While theological debates may ebb and flow, and questions may arise, the essence of baptism remains constant—a declaration of faith, a response to God's grace, and an invitation to partake in the divine drama of death and resurrection.

As we part ways with these turbulent waters, let us remember that baptism is not merely a ritual but a profound journey of faith. It is an act that symbolizes our entry into the body of Christ, our cleansing from sin, and our commitment to follow in His footsteps. In a world of ever-changing tides, the waters of baptism stand as a steadfast reminder of God's unchanging love and His desire to draw us into His eternal river of grace.

May the insights gained from our exploration of baptismal controversies and challenges serve as a compass, guiding you through the depths of your own faith journey. As you navigate these waters, may you find clarity, conviction, and a deeper connection to the transformative power of God's grace. And may you always be drenched in the faith that flows from the source of living water, Jesus Christ, our Lord and Savior.

Afterword

Where Do We Go from Here?

A s we come to the closing chapter of "Drenched in Faith: The Transformative Act of Water Baptism," the second installment in The Living Waters Series, I want to express my heartfelt gratitude for embarking on this journey of exploration with me. Together, we have navigated the flowing waters of baptism, unraveling its profound significance and timeless relevance.

In the prequel, "Passion for Christ: New Beginnings," we ignited the flames of devotion, laying the foundation for the deeper spiritual understanding we've gained in this book. From the inception of our faith to the culmination of the baptismal experience, our quest has been to uncover the wellsprings of divine truth that run deep within the Christian tradition.

In this Living Waters Series, we have embarked on a quest to dive deeper into the spiritual currents that flow through the Christian faith. From the prequel, "Passion for Christ: New Beginnings," which kindled the fire of devotion, to the depths of baptism in this book, we have sought to understand the source of our faith and the transformative power it holds.

Where Do We Go from Here?

As we cast our gaze towards the next chapter in The Living Waters Series, "Spirit Filled Life: The Unseen Force of Divine Power," we continue our odyssey into the mysteries of faith. This book will lead us into the realm of the Holy Spirit—the unseen yet omnipresent force that empowers and guides us on our Christian pilgrimage. The Spirit is like the wind, blowing where it wills; it is like a never-ending river, quenching our spiritual thirst; and it is like a refining fire, purifying our souls. In the upcoming pages, we will explore how to walk in harmony with this divine presence and embrace the fullness of a spirit-filled life.

However, let us not forget that our journey of faith extends far beyond the boundaries of these pages. It is a lifelong expedition, a ceaseless exploration of the boundless depths of God's love and grace. As we move forward, let us do so with hearts open to fresh revelations, minds eager to grapple with deeper truths, and souls firmly anchored in the unshakable foundation of Christ.

May The Living Waters Series continue to serve as a source of inspiration, reflection, and spiritual growth for you. And may your faith, like a mighty river, continue to flow, nourishing your soul and quenching your thirst for a more profound understanding of the divine.

Thank you for embarking on this incredible journey with me. Until we meet again in the next installment, may your faith be drenched in the living waters of God's unfailing love and boundless grace.

With profound gratitude and blessings,

Lori Ann Moeszinger

Bibliography

The Living Waters Series

In the quest to explore the depths of what it truly means to be a follower of Christ, the journey often leads us to the wisdom of many who have walked the path before us. "Passion for Christ: New Beginnings," along with its ten resulting volumes in The Living Waters Series, and then, "In sacred Conversation: The New Testament Prayer Guide" stands as a beacon, illuminating the various facets of Christian living.

The bibliography presented herein is not merely a list; it is a tapestry woven from the threads of countless believers, theologians, historians, and spiritual leaders whose insights and experiences have been invaluable in shaping the discourse within these pages. It serves as an atlas, guiding the earnest seeker through the landscapes of thought that have been traversed to bring these works to fruition.

Each book has been carefully selected to enrich understanding, to challenge preconceptions, and to offer solace and strength on this pilgrimage we embark upon in our daily lives. They are not just citations but conversations with the past, dialogues with the divine, and intersections with ideas that compel us towards a deeper, more profound faith.

As you peruse this bibliography, may it be more than a reference. May it become a repository of knowledge, a companion in study, and gateway to an ever-expanding world of theological richness and spiritual depth. Here lies the foundation upon which The Living Waters Series is built— each book contributing to the symphony of voices that call us to live out faith with vigor and sincerity.

May this bibliography serve you as your guide and inspiration, beckoning you to further exploration, deeper understanding, and a more passionate pursuit of the One who calls us to new beginnings.

The Living Waters Series

The Living Waters Series is a beacon for all those navigating the depths of Christian faith. Encompassing a collection of twelve transformative works, including the cornerstone overview, "Passion for Christ: New Beginnings," this series is a comprehensive journey through the core tenets of

Christianity. From the awakening of the soul to the embrace of eternity, each book delves into critical aspects of belief, practice, and divine experience. Readers are offered a wellspring of wisdom on salvation, baptism, filled with the Holy Spirit, Scripture, church community, tithing, giving, praying for unsaved loved ones, evangelism, and living a life that echoes beyond time. Crafted for both new believers and seasoned disciples, The Living Waters Series stands as a testament to the enduring power of faith and the relentless love of God that flows through every page.

Passion for Christ: New Beginning

Moeszinger, Lori Ann. Passion for Christ: New Beginnings. The Ridge Publishing Group, August 2024.

In her poignant and insightful book, "Passion for Christ: New Beginnings," Lori Ann Moeszinger embarks on an in-depth exploration of transformative Christian living, providing a vital resource for both new converts and long-standing believers seeking to renew their faith. As the first installment of The Living Waters Series, this volume not only introduces readers to the fundamental principles of living a Christ-centered life but also guides them through the practical aspects of incorporating these principles into daily activities and decisions.

Moeszinger adeptly combines theological depth with accessible writing to address the challenges of maintaining spiritual integrity in the modern world. With each chapter, she carefully unpacks the virtues of a life surrendered to Christ, using scriptural references and personal anecdotes to enhance the reader's understanding and application of biblical teachings. This book is an essential guide for anyone committed to pursuing a deep, authentic relationship with God through Jesus Christ, promising not just spiritual insights but a transformative journey of the heart and soul.

Faith On Trial:
The Startling Reality of Genuine Belief

Moeszinger, Lori Ann. Faith On Trial: The Startling Reality of Genuine Belief. The Living Waters Series. The Ridge Publishing Group, September 2024.

Lori Ann Moeszinger's "Faith On Trial: The Startling Reality of Genuine Belief" serves as the opening volume of The Living Waters Series, inviting readers into a compelling journey through the depths of authentic Christian faith. This book confronts essential questions about the nature of belief, the essence of grace, and the rigor of salvation with an unflinching clarity that is both challenging and enlightening.

Structured around critical examinations of foundational Christian doctrines—such as the Roman Road and the Four Spiritual Laws—"Faith On Trial" offers readers a rigorous pathway to assess and affirm the authenticity of their faith. Through thoughtful analysis and personal introspection,

Moeszinger encourages believers to scrutinize their spiritual convictions against biblical standards, providing a comprehensive guide to understanding and embracing a genuine Christian life.

Each chapter in "Faith On Trial" is designed not only to inform but to transform, urging readers to consider deeply the eternal implications of their faith and their readiness to stand before God. This book is a must-read for anyone seeking to deepen their spiritual understanding and to live out a faith that truly withstands the trials and tribulations of modern life.

Drenched in Faith:
The Transformative Act of Water Baptism

Moeszinger, Lori Ann. Drenched in Faith: The Transformative Act of Water Baptism. The Living Waters Series. The Ridge Publishing Group, October 2024.

In the second installment of The Living Waters Series, Lori Ann Moeszinger offers a profound exploration into the spiritual significance of baptism in "Drenched in Faith: The Transformative Act of Water Baptism." This book navigates through the historical, symbolic, and deeply personal aspects of baptism, presenting it as a crucial rite of passage for believers.

Moeszinger delves into the roots of baptism from its biblical origins to its modern-day applications, exploring how this ancient ritual acts as a bridge between personal faith and communal identity. The book provides a thorough investigation into whether baptism is merely a symbolic act or a necessary step towards salvation, examining its role in shaping Christian identity across the ages.

Each chapter of "Drenched in Faith" is designed to engage readers with theological insights and spiritual reflections, encouraging them to consider how baptism's transformative power can impact their own lives and the lives of those around them. From the cleansing waters of the Jordan River to the sacred spaces of contemporary churches, Moeszinger invites readers to rediscover baptism as a dynamic and ongoing act of faith that continues to resonate with profound spiritual significance.

This book is essential for anyone seeking to deepen their understanding of a foundational Christian practice. It challenges believers to rethink the role of baptism within the broader context of their spiritual journey, making it a vital resource for those looking to embrace a life truly drenched in faith.

Spirit Filled Life:
The Unseen Force of Divine Power

Moeszinger, Lori Ann. Spirit Filled Life: The Unseen Force of Divine Power. The Living Waters Series. The Ridge Publishing Group, November 2024.

In the third installment of The Living Waters Series, Lori Ann Moeszinger takes readers on a profound journey into the supernatural realms of Christianity in "Spirit Filled Life: The Unseen Force of Divine Power." This book provides a comprehensive exploration of the Holy Spirit's dynamic role in the believer's life, from the dramatic events of Pentecost to the subtle guidances in daily living.

Moeszinger offers deep biblical insights, historical contexts, and personal testimonies to illustrate the transformative impact of being filled with the Holy Spirit. The book discusses various manifestations of the Holy Spirit, such as speaking in tongues and prophetic insights, and distinguishes between public expressions of faith and intimate spiritual experiences.

Each chapter is designed not only to inform but also to inspire and challenge readers to invite the Holy Spirit more fully into their lives. Moeszinger encourages a deeper engagement with the Spirit's power, promising readers a renewed sense of faith and a more profound understanding of God's presence.

"Spirit Filled Life" serves as both a theological guide and a practical manual for those seeking to enhance their spiritual journey through Holy Spirit empowerment. It is an essential resource for anyone wishing to explore the breadth and depth of the Spirit's work in their life and to experience the full potential of living a Spirit-empowered life.

The Bible Unbound:
Trust, Translation, and Transformation

Moeszinger, Lori Ann. The Bible Unbound: Trust, Translation, and Transformation. The Living Waters Series. The Ridge Publishing Group, December 2024.

In the fourth installment of The Living Waters Series, Lori Ann Moeszinger delivers a compelling exploration of the Bible in "The Bible Unbound: Trust, Translation, and Transformation." This book offers readers an in-depth look into the authenticity of Bible translations, the interpretation of prophecy, and the application of biblical truths to modern life.

Moeszinger expertly guides readers through the complex landscape of Scripture, addressing common misconceptions and highlighting the enduring relevance of the Bible. Through a blend of scholarly research and accessible writing, she explores how accurate translations impact our understanding of ancient texts and unpacks the most enigmatic prophecies with clarity.

Each chapter of "The Bible Unbound" serves as both a lesson in biblical scholarship and a testament to the transformative power of Scripture. Moeszinger encourages readers to delve deeper into their faith by engaging with the Bible in a way that is both informed and passionate. This book is an essential resource for anyone seeking to deepen their understanding of Scripture and its application to their daily lives, providing the tools needed to navigate the rich terrain of biblical teachings and to embrace the Bible's transformative power in personal and communal contexts.

"The Bible Unbound" is more than a guide; it is an invitation to experience the Bible as a living, breathing entity that offers renewal and guidance for believers seeking to align their lives with eternal truths. This work is an indispensable part of any Christian's library, offering profound insights that promise to enrich the reader's spiritual journey and understanding of their faith.

Prophets and Pulpits: Discerning Truth in the House of God

Moeszinger, Lori Ann. Prophets and Pulpits: Discerning Truth in the House of God. The Living Waters Series. The Ridge Publishing Group, January 2025.

In the fifth volume of The Living Waters Series, Lori Ann Moeszinger delivers a probing examination of modern church practices and prophetic claims in "Prophets and Pulpits: Discerning Truth in the House of God." This book challenges believers to cultivate a discerning spirit towards spiritual leadership and worship, encouraging a return to Scripture-based truth and authenticity.

Moeszinger navigates through the intricate landscape of contemporary Christian worship, offering a critical look at how cultural customs intersect with and often obscure biblical doctrines. The book addresses hot-button issues such as the validity of modern prophetic voices, the authenticity of church practices, and the origins of commonly accepted Christian holidays like Christmas, providing a balanced perspective rooted in solid theological research.

"Prophets and Pulpits" serves not only as an educational resource but also as a guide for personal and communal spiritual growth. Moeszinger equips readers with the tools necessary to discern genuine biblical teachings from prevalent myths, promoting a deeper understanding of what it means to engage in genuine worship and follow godly leadership.

The book is a vital resource for anyone seeking to deepen their knowledge of church doctrine and enhance their worship experience. It is particularly useful for those wishing to understand the nuances of prophetic claims and the dynamics of spiritual authority within the context of modern Christianity.

Through engaging narrative and rigorous analysis, "Prophets and Pulpits" offers a transformative look at the essentials of a robust Christian faith, making it an indispensable addition to any believer's library who is eager to ensure their faith practices are grounded in truth and aligned with the teachings of Scripture.

Beyond the Tithe:
The Transformative Power of Generous Faith

Moeszinger, Lori Ann. Beyond the Tithe: The Transformative Power of Generous Faith. The Living Waters Series. The Ridge Publishing Group, February 2025.

In the sixth installment of The Living Waters Series, Lori Ann Moeszinger takes readers on a profound journey in "Beyond the Tithe: The Transformative Power of Generous Faith," exploring the spiritual richness that emerges from transcending traditional tithing practices. This volume challenges and encourages readers to redefine their understanding of generosity and its profound impact on both the giver and the receiver.

Delving into the biblical foundations of giving and its implications for modern believers, Moeszinger expertly weaves together scriptural insights, personal stories, and theological reflections to illustrate how generosity extends far beyond monetary contributions. She explores the joy and spiritual growth that come from a life characterized by giving, urging readers to embrace a more expansive view of generosity as a core element of Christian faith.

"Beyond the Tithe" not only discusses the historical and biblical context of tithing but also encourages a deeper, more intentional practice of generosity. Through compelling narrative and actionable advice, Moeszinger inspires readers to integrate generosity into their daily lives as a means of fostering spiritual development and enriching their communities.

This book serves as an essential guide for anyone seeking to deepen their spiritual journey through the practice of generous living. It is an invaluable resource for understanding how the act of giving can transform lives, build lasting legacies, and reflect the love of Christ in tangible ways.

Join Lori Ann Moeszinger in discovering the transformative power of generosity and learn how expanding your practice of giving can lead to a richer, more fulfilling faith journey.

Heart of Abundance:
The Journey to Radical Giving and Receiving

Moeszinger, Lori Ann. Heart of Abundance: The Journey to Radical Giving and Receiving. The Living Waters Series. The Ridge Publishing Group, March 2025.

In the seventh book of The Living Waters Series, Lori Ann Moeszinger leads readers into the enriching world of generosity in "Heart of Abundance: The Journey to Radical Giving and Receiving." This volume delves into the transformative power of generosity, exploring how radical giving and receiving can fundamentally enrich one's life and spirit.

Moeszinger expertly combines compelling narratives with profound biblical insights, illustrating how the acts of giving and receiving are not just transactions but transformative experiences that reflect divine love and foster deep personal fulfillment. Through stories of individuals and communities engaging in acts of unprecedented generosity, the book inspires readers to open their hearts and extend their hands in ways that leave lasting impacts.

"Heart of Abundance" challenges its readers to rethink traditional perceptions of generosity and to embrace a lifestyle of abundant giving that aligns with biblical teachings. It encourages a holistic view of generosity that transcends mere material giving and receives, promoting a life enriched by spiritual depth and communal connection.

This book is an essential resource for anyone seeking to deepen their understanding of spiritual abundance and to practice generosity in transformative ways. It provides practical guidance and inspiring examples that equip readers to start their own journey of radical generosity, aiming to cultivate a legacy of love and purpose that resonates through their lives and beyond.

Join Lori Ann Moeszinger in "Heart of Abundance" to discover how embracing radical generosity can lead you to a life filled with joy, purpose, and abundant fulfillment.

Heaven's Reach: Drawing the Unbelieving into the Fold

Moeszinger, Lori Ann. Heaven's Reach: Drawing the Unbelieving into the Fold. The Living Waters Series. The Ridge Publishing Group, April 2025.

In the eighth book of The Living Waters Series, Lori Ann Moeszinger tackles the profound power of intercessory prayer in "Heaven's Reach: Drawing the Unbelieving into the Fold." This volume delves into the spiritual practice of interceding for those who have not yet embraced faith, exploring the transformative impact such prayers can have on both the individual and the wider community.

Moeszinger expertly combines theological insights with practical advice, providing readers with a comprehensive guide to intercessory prayer. Through compelling stories and a deep biblical understanding, she illustrates how strategic and compassionate prayer can bridge the gap between skepticism and faith, transforming doubts into devotion and indifference into fervor.

"Heaven's Reach" is designed to empower readers to cultivate a deeper compassion for the unbelieving and to engage in the mission of evangelism through prayer. The book is a call to action, encouraging believers to take up the mantle of intercessors, fostering a legacy of faith that reaches beyond personal boundaries and into the hearts of those around them.

This installment is an essential resource for anyone looking to deepen their understanding of evangelistic prayer and its role in drawing the unbelieving into a life of faith. It offers not just knowledge, but also the tools needed for readers to become active participants in what Moeszinger describes as "the greatest commission given to mankind."

Join Lori Ann Moeszinger in "Heaven's Reach" to discover the profound joy and fulfillment that comes from engaging in the transformative power of prayer and witness the change it can bring to the world.

Breaking Silence:
The Charge to Uphold the Faith Out Loud

Moeszinger, Lori Ann. Breaking Silence: The Charge to Uphold the Faith Out Loud. The Living Waters Series. The Ridge Publishing Group, May 2025.

In the ninth book of The Living Waters Series, Lori Ann Moeszinger delivers a compelling call to action with "Breaking Silence: The Charge to Uphold the Faith Out Loud." This installment challenges believers to vocalize their faith boldly and effectively, transforming them from silent observers to vocal advocates for Christ in a world desperate for truth.

Through a blend of scriptural wisdom and actionable advice, Moeszinger equips readers to navigate the complexities of modern evangelism. She tackles the barriers that often keep Christians silent, offering strategies to overcome fear and resistance while encouraging a dynamic expression of faith that resonates in both personal interactions and broader societal engagement.

"Breaking Silence" serves as both a guide and an inspiration for Christians eager to make their faith audible in the cacophony of global discourse. It provides practical steps for engaging in vocal faith advocacy, emphasizing the importance of truth spoken with love and conviction. Moeszinger's insightful guidance helps readers harness the power of their voice to bridge gaps, heal divisions, and lead others toward the transformative power of the Gospel.

This book is an essential tool for anyone ready to take their faith expression to the next level, offering both the why and the how of effective communication. Prepare to be inspired, challenged, and equipped to make your faith heard in a world yearning for hope and direction.

Join Lori Ann Moeszinger in a movement that not only breaks the silence but also builds a legacy of faith that echoes through eternity.

Beyond the Final Breath:
The Christian's Voyage into Eternity

Moeszinger, Lori Ann. Beyond the Final Breath: The Christian's Voyage into Eternity. The Living Waters Series. The Ridge Publishing Group, June 2025.

In the monumental finale of The Living Waters Series, Lori Ann Moeszinger provides readers with a profound exploration into the Christian perspective on life after death in "Beyond the Final Breath: The Christian's Voyage into Eternity." This book serves as a spiritual guide, offering deep biblical insights and thoughtful inquiries into the mysteries of the afterlife and the soul's journey beyond mortal existence.

Through a blend of scriptural interpretation and reflective exploration, Moeszinger challenges readers to consider the profound questions surrounding our eternal destiny. She navigates through complex theological terrain with clarity and compassion, addressing topics such as the nature of the eternal body, the significance of the Lamb's Book of Life, and what Scripture reveals about the afterlife.

"Beyond the Final Breath" is crafted not only to inform but also to inspire readers to align their earthly lives with God's eternal promises. It encourages a life that views its conclusion not as an end but as the commencement of a glorious, eternal existence. This book is an indispensable resource for anyone seeking to understand the biblical teachings on eternity and how they apply to personal faith and the broader Christian hope.

Join Lori Ann Moeszinger in this culminating volume as she guides you through the Christian eternal journey, preparing you for a life beyond death filled with hope and glory. This is more than just a book—it is a beacon for all who seek to live their earthly lives in anticipation of their eternal home.

In Sacred Conversation: Getting Your Prayer Life In Order

Moeszinger, Lori Ann. In Sacred Conversation: Getting Your Prayer Life In Order. The Living Waters Series Sequel. The Ridge Publishing Group, July 2025.

As a sequel to the widely acclaimed The Living Waters Series, Lori Ann Moeszinger's "In Sacred Conversation: Getting Your Prayer Life In Order" offers readers an insightful and practical guide to mastering the art of prayer according to New Testament principles. This book explores ten fundamental prayers, elucidating their significance and application in the daily lives of believers, aiming to deepen their communion with God.

The guide is meticulously structured to enhance the reader's understanding of effective prayer, incorporating scriptural foundations and practical steps to develop a disciplined prayer routine. Moeszinger integrates biblical insights with contemporary relevance, making each lesson accessible and actionable for modern Christians seeking to fortify their prayer lives.

"In Sacred Conversation" is designed not only to educate but also to transform, encouraging readers to integrate prayer seamlessly into their daily routine, thus enriching their spiritual journey and relationship with God. It serves as an essential resource for anyone eager to enhance their communication with the divine, providing the tools needed for a more profound, effective spiritual practice.

This sequel continues the tradition of The Living Waters Series by guiding readers through a detailed exploration of biblical teachings, encouraging them to live out their faith with confidence and sincerity. Ideal for both new and seasoned believers, "In Sacred Conversation" is more than just a book—it's a spiritual mentor for all who seek to align their prayer life with God's eternal promises.

Author Photo © 2023 Edwin Wolfe

LORI ANN MOESZINGER, affectionately known as "L," stands at the creative helm of The Ridge Publishing Group and its diverse imprints. A prolific American author, insightful blogger, and dynamic publisher, she crafts words that resonate and narratives that captivate. Now, nestled in the scenic tranquility of Coeur d'Alene, Idaho, Lori finds inspiration in the lakeside whispers and the companionship of her husband and their two beloved dogs.

Her writing journey traverses various pseudonyms, each a distinct facet of her expansive expertise. As Ann Patterson, she delves into the intricacies of business law, distilling complex concepts into clear, actionable advice. Under the byline L. A. Moeszinger, she navigates the nuanced realms of writing, marketing, and publishing, guiding aspiring authors toward their dreams. In her biblical and personal writings, she embraces her full name, Lori Ann Moeszinger, offering reflections steeped in faith and introspection.

Yet, it's through the New Youniversity Chronicles, The Manhattan Diaries series that Lori's versatility truly shines, showcasing her storytelling prowess across a spectrum of voices, each as engaging and unique as the last. Her foundational belief in faith's power, the virtue of blessings, and the virtues of industrious dedication pulses through every line she writes.

Transcending her former life as a lawyer, Lori now revels in the freedom of expression that authorship and publishing afford—a stark contrast to the rigid confines of law. Her new chapter is one marked by a fervent passion for empowering others, a commitment to hard work, and the joy of sharing her literary gifts.

Discover the multifaced worlds Lori has woven at her websites and blog sites, or connect with her on her social media platforms where she continues to inspire, educate, and transform the written word into a shared experience of growth and discovery.

Parent Website: https://www.RidgePublishingGroup.com and

    blog site https://www.PublisherAndHerWorld.com

Publisher Website: https://www.GuardiansofBiblicalTruth.com and

    blog site https://www.Jesus-Says.com

Author website: https://www.LAMoeszinger.com and New Youniversity sites:

https://www.NewYouniversity.com,
https://www.ManhattanChronicles.com

Bridge Website: https://www.AuthorsDoor.com and

blog site https://www.AuthorsRedDoor.com

Entertainment website: https://www.EthanFoxBooks.com and

blog site https://www.KidsStagram.com

Want More?

Welcome to Coffee with God! Jesus-Says.com! Dive into our blog for inspiring insights and biblical truths that deepen your faith and enrich your spiritual journey. Explore thought-provoking articles, personal testimonies, and practical guidance rooted in Scripture. Whether you're new to the faith or a lifelong believer, Jesus-Says offers wisdom and encouragement for your walk with Christ. Join our community and grow in your relationship with God!

Guardians of Biblical Truth Hub

Welcome to our Guardians of Biblical Truth Facebook page! Join our community to deepen your understanding of the Bible and live out its principles. Engage in enriching Bible studies, share faith testimonies, and connect with like-minded believers. Whether you're new to the faith or a seasoned believer, you'll find support and inspiration here. Join us today and grow in your walk with Christ.

Guardians of Biblical Truth Forum

Welcome to our Guardians of Biblical Truth Forum! Join our closed Facebook group to deepen your understanding of the Bible and strengthen your faith. Engage in enriching discussions, share personal testimonies, and connect with a supportive community of believers. Whether you're new to the faith or a seasoned believer, you'll find inspiration and encouragement here. Join us today and grow in your walk with Christ!

www.ingramcontent.com/pod-product-compliance
Lightning Source LLC
Chambersburg PA
CBHW021622120626
46545CB00001B/357